Transition: Life's Unavoidable Reality

A Guide to Successfully Navigating Change

Robert Mitchell, MACL

ISBN: 978-0692638408

Note to the Reader

I do not possess the adequate vocabulary to describe just how much my wife Lisa and our three daughters Madison, Meghan, and Marley mean to me. They truly are my life. This book is for each one of them. It's our story and I love you.

Contents

Introduction

Transitions are a constant in life. Everyone experiences them, individually and collectively, in areas such as: education, marriage, parenthood, divorce, relocations, jobs, retirement and disease. This reality has the potential to cause us either an unbearable amount of stress or incalculable benefits. There is no way to go through life without facing a barrage of transitional events.

Every transition has the potential to stop you from living out your dreams, causing you to arrive at the end of your life with tremendous regrets. Our natural tendency is to accept things as they are, with the belief that there's no way to relieve the anxiety associated with those transitions.

What's the number one dilemma associated with transition? It's that we don't inherently possess a default Global Positioning System (GPS) to successfully navigate through change. We need directions to know how to get through the emotional, intellectual, physical, and spiritual changes.

In the midst of transitions, everyone wants to know, "How do I successfully get from here, where it's no longer comfortable, to there, a better place?" Where can I get help to walk through this inescapable experience in my life? Imagine facing tomorrow free from the stress associated with inescapable transitions. Imagine getting practical knowledge on how to effectively approach this challenge.

This book is my perspective on a few specific areas of transition. My goal is to offer hope to those who are enduring the pressure brought on by transition, who know someone who is feeling overwhelmed, or who want to be equipped for what's coming next in their life.

My experiences have helped me learn some of the telltale signs when a transition is approaching. Being able to recognize these indicators is vital. I'll reveal some clues in the following chapters. Then, once you're familiar with what's coming, you'll need to know the key steps to employ in order to pass through each transitional season better. Far too often, these life passages leave us confused, so I hope you'll find the steps I provide to be helpful for you.

On a midmorning flight from Denver to Houston, ironically, while working on this introduction, I saw an in-flight magazine ad with the headline: "Every Flight Has a Navigator. So Should Every Cancer Patient."

That statement resonated with me for two reasons: my passion for writing a book about transition to help people navigate intense moments in their lives, and the reference to cancer, because of the two times my mother battled this disease.

The advertisement went on to say:

> Sarah Cannon. Fighting Cancer Together. A global leader in cancer research and treatment. Sarah Cannon brings together innovative medical minds and unparalleled resources to advance therapies and deliver personalized care. Through our cancer programs located across the United States and United Kingdom, we connect each patient with a nurse navigator, specialized in cancer care, to provide one-on-one guidance and support through every aspect of their journey. We understand the power of fighting cancer together. No one should go

through it alone. Visit FightingCancerTogether.com to learn more.

This says everything you need to know right now about transition. As your "navigator," I promise you are not alone and your life does have meaning.

Although no one person has the answer for every situation, I have personal experience with transition, as you will see in the stories to come, and my entire life has been marked by one transition after another. I'm certain the examples I share are not unique to me and I hope what I learned while traveling though those times will be insightful for you.

My goal is to share what I know about transition and to walk alongside you, the reader, to give you immediate assistance. You are not alone on this journey. As you will see in the following chapters, I've been there, done that, and got the T-shirt a few times!

There's no point in living ill-equipped for transition and on the verge of catastrophe. If you're tired of being stuck, confused, frustrated, and scared about making it, then let this book be the motivation you need to jump right into the middle of what you're facing with a workable plan for success, so you'll be positioned correctly when the next season of change comes. Then you can be at a place where you no longer dread the next move.

You can do it! You've got this! You'll be ready!

Keynote speaker, success coach and best-selling author Mitch Matthews said, "If you're working with me then you're already inspired, the thing we've got to do is transition to action."

At the end of each chapter, I've presented one or more action steps you can take, to help you apply the principles you've learned and to help you "transition to action." They are presented in summary form here in the book, but if you want the detailed version of the action steps, you can download my **FREE PDF: "41 Action Steps to Prepare for and Get Through Transition."** This report is absolutely free and is my way of saying thank you for reading this book. You can download it here: http://transitionbook.info

I join with Mitch in saying, "Work with me, and, by all means, take action right now. Read this book; it will pay high dividends in the days to come."

I sincerely believe that your life will be enhanced and your despair minimalized when you read and apply the principles in these chapters. Life is about navigating transitions with confidence, balance, and resolve. To succeed at this, you need support, strength, and knowledge.

Addressing, not avoiding, transitional reality brings clarity of existence. And that is precisely what I'm offering you in this book. Are you ready? Then, let's get started!

Section I—Lessons Learned by a Stream

1. A New World

Transition was taking place under the water, on the water, and above the water.

Sleep always eludes me when the excitement of the coming morning enters my mind. It could be adrenaline, but, at any rate, it always plays out the same. I hurry to bed hoping to fall asleep quickly, being fully aware that the alarm will sound in a few short hours. The routine is much the same no matter the circumstances.

First, I lie awake forever, unable to shut my brain down. Second, I drift off and wake up a thousand times with the plaguing thought, "Is it time yet?" Then when it finally is time to get up, I usually start the day startled and dead tired from a long night of tossing and turning.

A life-changing hobby

The sun was hiding and would remain hidden for a while, leaving the cool night air to hang on as long as possible. When the wake-up call suddenly erupted, my feet labored to catch up with the accelerated rate of my heart. Grabbing the stuff strategically laid out the night before; I rushed out the door, not wanting to be late.

Driving up, I saw a light coming out of a doorway on the south side of the Hunter Banks building. My guide for the day was in a back room gathering the equipment we would need for this memorable outing. It was my first "for real" fly-fishing adventure.

When I walked in, "What size shoe do you wear?" was one of the first questions he asked. I can only remember a couple other things he said, like, "What about your license?" and "Have you done this before?" Not much for small talk. He obviously had a get-to-the-point, get-it-done, let's-get-out-of-here mentality.

In his truck a few minutes later, I could sense he was going over a mental checklist: waders, boots, rods, reels, flies, drinks, lunches, snacks, rain gear, license, tippet, indicators, net, floatants, hats, sunscreen, vests, leaders, pliers, weights, and more. One thing this guy forgot to check off his list was the exorbitant amount of questions I would ask the following eight hours! That early-morning, ninety-minute drive to the water went by quickly as we worked our way through the awkwardness of introductions.

Knowing when to move

It took precious moments to get all rigged up while standing in the parking area before taking our brief hike, and the sun was just rising as we slipped down to the edge of the Davidson River.

I remember the air being clean and the temperature crisp that morning in the Pisgah National Forest. (And after this adventure, Brevard, a picturesque town in Western North Carolina became a favorite place of mine.)

We stood there, dressed in the finest of Gore-Tex waders, felt bottom boots, and, with a plethora of fly-fishing equipment in hand. Everything seemed to be in place, we were fully equipped, but for some strange reason, not hurrying into the moving water.

To the untrained and inexperienced eye like mine that day, the stream represented nothing more than fast moving water crashing over rocks, banks, and branches. But to the "already-been-there-done-that" guide, there was something of greater importance happening in that little swath of liquid real estate.

I was unaware of it, but life was transpiring within a few feet of where we were standing. And the opportunity for success or failure depended greatly upon our knowledge of that life. The "professional" was aware, dialed in, and patient. The "newbie" was unsuspecting, clueless, and anxious.

When you don't know what you don't know

It's interesting how two people of similar age and enthusiasm can look at life from the same vantage point but see things completely differently. These unique perspectives are based on each individual's knowledge and past encounters. One person observes particulars and specifics, while the other person just sees the obvious and the generalities.

Right now there are events transpiring in your life that someone else would see and approach exactly the opposite of you. There's nothing wrong with that, unless you fail to realize that there are important keys you're not familiar with. The pressing question is,

"Am I willing to start looking from a more informed perspective or be content to continue seeing with limited understanding?"

What I eventually realized, impatiently waiting on that laurel-covered riverbank, was incredible transitions were happening right before my unsuspecting eyes. I just wasn't observant or knowledgeable enough to understand it, at first.

My guide was formulating an effective plan to take advantage of those transitions. I, on the other hand, was caught up in the gadgetry of a new hobby and the adrenaline induced drive to catch a fish. What the guide knew, but I didn't, was that there were transitions happening in three specific places, yet irrefutably connected.

- **Under** the water

- **On** the water

- **Above** the water.

You'll read about those places throughout this book, so you'll want to remember them.

Learning what I didn't know

I had no idea that fly-fishing would require the understanding of an entomologist, knowledge of a botanist, skill of a mariner, and ability of a professional tightrope walker. Humorous as it seems, I was lacking the tools all the way around. Thankfully, the guy beside me was in his element.

Having experienced this before, my friend-for-the-day knew where I was and stepped up to help me achieve fly-fishing success. After studying the signs discerned by his trained eye, it was finally time to "match the hatch." After tying the perfect fly on my line we slipped into the current and he showed me how to produce an irresistible presentation. It felt like the weight of the world rode on each of my casts.

Quickly, I realized several fly-fishing truths:

1. Awkward waders are necessary when the water temperature is low.

2. Felt bottom boots are a lifesaver when attempting to stand on slippery river rocks.

3. The weight of a size #19 fly is substantially different than heavy crank bait.

Suddenly, a small ring of water spread out in all directions about 20 feet in front of us.

"Did you see that?" my guide whispered.

"See what?" I asked.

"That fish," he said pointing.

"Where?" I said, not seeing a fish.

"Right there in front of you," he said.

"Cast right there," was the last thing I heard, until I totally missed the mark. Truthfully, it was more laughable than successful. It still makes me laugh, when I think about how frustrated that guy must have been.

Oh, the triumph or defeat a ripple on the surface of life can provide!

Going deeper

At the end of my fly-line and tippet was an "Elk Hair Caddis." It was designed to entice fish in that particular setting. But I needed to get a handle on a few other things before I could actually catch a feeding trout.

The roll cast, proper drift, recognizing the feeding tendencies of an amazing creature, the feel of setting a hook, landing and releasing fish were all things I learned on that infamous stream. Reminiscing on this trip, I just realized that what actually got hooked was me, not many fish!

The art of fly-fishing has brought me a lot of pleasure and, at the same time, caused me to see other areas of life differently. That day, instead of just catching fish, I was introduced to the importance of understanding the life cycle of an aquatic insect if I wanted to be a successful fly-fisherman.

In the next chapter you'll learn how my fly-fishing adventure helped me to understand the experience of transition.

***

Action Step #1: Let go and get in the flow.

2. Defining Transition

"We are living at the very beginning of a huge shift with regards to human existence, and it isn't all good."

—*Randy Frazee*, Making Room for Life

Transitions are a reality of life. No one can escape them, so it's important to understand, accept, and prepare for them. I've often wondered why more hasn't been written about it, especially since coming to grips with transition is an overlooked "ingredient" to a better life.

My iPhone dictionary defines transition like this:

Transition: (noun) 1) movement, passage, or change from one position, stage, state, subject, concept, etc., to another; change: the transition from adolescence to adulthood.

The importance of perspective

Social media guru and author Bruce Van Horn said, "In a crisis, we want answers. Answers often don't come until later. What we need in a crisis is perspective." *Perspective* is an important concept to consider when looking at transition. And without honest perspective, you can forget successfully navigating change.

How you see things makes a big difference in how those things turn out. It's important to search for a broad view of your circumstance

See the forest, not the tree

since a limited view creates tension and overwhelming feelings of hopelessness.

Change is everywhere

All around us are visible signs of change. Randy Frazee reveals this in his book, *Making Room for Life*, where he writes about the agricultural lifestyle of the last several thousand years. He said, "We are living at the very beginning of a huge shift with regards to human existence, and it isn't all good. In 1913, farm products accounted for 70% of world trade. Today, it accounts for only 17%." This cultural change thrust us into accepting a new reality, with many benefits of the past now gone and new challenges to address.

From a big picture perspective, people are naturally, environmentally, and socially conditioned for transitions, by one constant, "change." If that's true, then why are we always surprised and a step behind when those shifts occur?

Everyday life constantly presents new adventures, possibilities, and opportunities. We accept seasonal change by adjusting our activities and clothing. Education is full of change, from preschool to college. In every election cycle, politicians talk about change and the country follows along expectantly. Through each one we move with a certain level of ease. All through our lives, we're presented with change, and it's not unfamiliar to us, yet we find certain types of transitions to be difficult.

The truth is that the world exists in a state of flux. Little that you and I know is permanent. And, here's the good news: hidden deep inside of us is the ability to successfully navigate through change.

***

Action Step #2: Review a past transition from a different perspective and see the good that came out of it.

3. Entomology / Ento...What?

Living below your purpose doesn't have to be your reality.

A new professor was hired partway through my college career. He wasn't like any of the other teachers the students at my small private religious institution were accustomed to. We were intrigued because this instructor was previously the head of a department at Virginia Tech and his expertise didn't seem to fit the mold or context at this school of ministry. It was a prime example of something coming out of left field.

His hiring wasn't a problem particularly, it was just surprising. And what was surprising was that he seemed to adjust well to the new environment even though his previous career was based on the study of bugs! Entomology is the scientific name. I'm confident this was a concentration that most of us in that particular college knew nothing about.

Dr. Sidney Poe was unique, completely different from the usual theology professor, and the only person I knew who was proficient in the area of insect research. I now laugh when I remember the effect his hire had on many of my peers—and me. No wonder the governing leadership decided to bring in this man. There were quite a few "bugs" milling around the campus during those years. And I mean that literally and figuratively.

Professor Poe was well adept in Entomology years before my own fly-fishing adventures introduced me to the importance of aquatic lifecycles. I wish there was a way to go back to those college days and ask him a few insect-related questions! I'm sure, it would make me a better fisherman.

A whole new world

Like the world of Entomology, there are new worlds regularly available in our lives. Fellow travelers discover those places all the time. The truth is you and I haven't found some of them yet.

There's nothing inherently wrong with this, but it's important to understand that you can't afford to miss your own individual discoveries or your life will be stagnant and won't move forward productively. Don't take offense! Make the decision to change.

If all you know is what someone else has shared with you, not what you've personally experienced, you end up with a shallow, unfulfilled life. Of course there's nothing wrong with appreciating what you've learned from influential people, but if you only live vicariously through the experiences of others, you won't reach your own personal fulfillment.

I challenge you to be a present-day Christopher Columbus! Go and experience all the beneficial unknowns of life. Doing that doesn't discount the advice of others, but it helps you enjoy the best of their lessons and your own experiences at the same time. Personal quest coupled with the assistance of those who've walked their own path is the ideal equation. Embrace those new worlds with expectancy— not dread.

As the Disney song aptly states, it's "A Whole New World." You could be just one successful transition away from a brand new adventure, one that will open up a world of endless possibilities for you and your family. Don't shy away from the unknown; embrace it with anticipation.

I've learned that, many times, the adventure comes in the transition itself. Trying new things and owning alternate possibilities have enriched my life. I'm one of those people who determined, long ago, to take intentional advantage of things that come my way. I hope your glimpse at my personal journey in these pages will help you to realize that you don't have to live below your purpose. A rich and full life comes from actively pursuing the things you desire. You have a choice of either claiming or forfeiting your life's purpose. It's up to you.

***

Action Step #3: Try something new.

4. Scary Doesn't Have to Be the Reality

Life is not about how quickly you can get through it, but about purposefully taking one step at a time and making the best of the journey.

Do you remember those homemade bug boards in school? You know, the ones with all the ugly, scary-looking bugs pinned down on Styrofoam?

Wasn't it crazy the attention and "buzz" created around those projects? Catching nasty little insects was only half the fun. Pinning them down, dead or alive, was a big part of the excitement.

What about the chore of identifying each of them? No, not like Jim, Jill, John, or Jenny; but the official name that would catch the attention of the observer and beef up your grade. Admit it; you couldn't even pronounce those names, much less spell them!

I can still see those square white boards lined with colorful pins, marked by indistinct lettering. Believe it or not, there was an organizational approach, right? Not just a bunch of random creepy crawly things on a board. Whether organizing by type, color or size, addressing those particulars was a required part of the grade.

No matter what effort went into those displays, they were always interesting and frightening at first glance. Bugs in general, cause us to jump, run, and scream, even put ourselves in danger! They just weird us out no matter how many times we have seen them. But scary doesn't have to be the reality when you understand the process at work.

It's a bug's life

A bug's life can be broken up into stages of metamorphosis. Metamorphosis means "a change of form" and there are two different types of an insect life cycle, "incomplete metamorphosis" and "complete metamorphosis," which are defined as:

- Incomplete metamorphosis has three stages: Egg— Nymph—Adult.

- Complete metamorphosis has four stages: Egg—Larva— Pupa—Adult.

Insects, just like us, pass through childhood and adolescence on our way to adulthood. Through each of these changes, there are noticeable differences that are recognized by size, color, and differing abilities. Interestingly, fish like to feed on the insects at all of the stages at different times. The question for the fisherman then, is, what stage of metamorphosis are the aquatic insects in? Are they in their beginnings under the water, partially through their changes on the surface of the water, or completely finished and able to be above the water, flying away? The knowledgeable fisherman can offer the targeted trout exactly what they're hungry for.

No transition can be accomplished without movement. Bugs move from egg to adult one stage at a time. This is not a sit-back-and-everything-will-be-good type of negotiation. It's a deliberate step-by-step endeavor.

Putting a plan in place

I mentioned the importance of "reading the water" in the first chapter. This involves looking for shadows, currents, riffs, pools and many other indicators, all of which help you move deliberately and confidently into attack-mode. Sometimes, getting to that place involves sneaking, shuffling, stepping, and sliding along a riverbank or across slime-covered rocks. It's all about getting into the best position to snare a skittish fish—and sometimes, it's hard to just stay standing up against all the opposing factors, which I've failed to do many times—but that's another story!

Keeping your eye on the target while everything else is happening around you can be challenging, so in moments of pressure, you need to plan your approach and footing. If not, you will blow one opportunity after another. Life is not about how quickly you can get through it, but purposefully taking one step at a time, while making the best out of the journey. And you thought fly-fishing was a breeze!

Then, after you've found what seems to be the perfect place, there has to be life transition happening in the water or all of your efforts in negotiating the flow are useless. My buddy, Eugene Wilson and I once braved the dangers of a large body of water and caught nothing because there was no metamorphosis taking place in that location.

Don't hate the things that are beyond your control. Just have a plan in place to survive them. When you know this from the beginning, you can own what's offered and work with the parts that refuse to be possessed.

***

Action Step #4: In order to gain a true sense of self, we have to quiet the mind and go within. Meditate for a few minutes once a day at a time when you won't be disturbed.

Action Step #5: Take the first step to get through your transition.

Action Step #6: Take out an insurance plan for the emotional costs of transitions.

5. Dimensional Life

---

*Dealing thoroughly with life transitions is
paramount for progress.*

Track with me here, because I want to make a transition where you could get lost if you're not reading carefully. Life is made up of multiple dimensions. There are three specific dimensions that I want to expand on. These dimensions are:

1. Inward—what is fully engulfed, happening under the surface, and impossible to see clearly from the outside

2. Outward—what can be seen on the surface, partially free but still connected

3. Overarching—the activity above and totally independent of outside control

These three dimensions are present in every life transition and each one needs to be addressed, with necessary adjustments made. If that doesn't happen, the purpose of the transition isn't accomplished, and breakdown occurs.

Slow down, go back, and re-read that last part.

Ultimately, we desire the completion of this individual metamorphosis. No one wants to intentionally get waylaid somewhere on their journey from first being confronted with change to finally understanding and enjoying the results of life's transitions.

Dealing with more than one dimension

I want to remind you of the lesson I learned on that first fly-fishing trip. Changes were occurring under, on, and above the water. Microscopic bugs by the thousands were hatching, emerging, and flying away, right in front of me, and I had no clue.

A similar process holds true for you and me. Each time we're faced with a transition, we must deal purposely with three dimensions: body, soul, and spirit. Life's transitions affect us internally, externally, and in the uncontrollable. We all have to work with the emotional, physical, and overarching aspects of change. Understand this fact:

When change occurs, it happens in the totality of the person and often all at the same time.

If you're uncomfortable with dimensional understanding, you might find it hard to accept what is happening in all three realms of your life. Fortunately, you can train your senses to look for the vital indicators leading to a well balanced approach to transition. No matter what type of transition is happening, it's important to address it from a "whole person" posture.

No one can see the internal transitions, while external transitions are, of course, visible. Then, there are two distinct parts to the external. One is outward, or on the surface; the other is above—or something you have no control over. Since it is beyond your power, it doesn't make sense to be frustrated by trying to change it. Just disconnect from the parts you can't change.

By intentionally considering all three dimensions, you can navigate your life's transitions productively. The Bible writer Solomon used an example of someone observing the weather then making a decision based on that one dimension. "*He that observeth the wind shall not sow; and he that regardeth the clouds shall not reap*" (Ecc. 11:4, KJV). This incomplete approach resulted in someone neglecting sowing and reaping.

When making decisions during the transition times in your life, you need to address all three dimensions, without ignoring any of them.

***

Action Step #7: In your meditation time, reflect on past transitions that didn't go well. What loose ends still need to be addressed?

6. 3 Musketeers

No matter what the risk, it's imperative to complete the process to attain your full potential.

Never lose connection with the hidden man.

Incredible transformation takes place under the surface of the water in a freestone stream. The most successful fly fishers I've known possess a heightened awareness of this. Whether that is knowledge of the angulations on the river floor, various water patterns created by altering depths, rocks, turns, fluctuating temperature, speed of the flow or something as unassuming as visibility, these variables directly affect the aquatic insects' transition.

I personally find it fascinating to learn about how trout feast on this particular stage, but if you're not an entomologist or a hardcore fly-fishing enthusiast, you probably aren't that interested in the egg, pupa, nymph, larva, or emergent, so I'll spare you the details. I'll just mention that these designations are important because they represent birth and the beginning of change.

Change happens in an inward place that reflects a part of us not seen from the outside. The hidden stuff going on underneath, such as our initial feelings and thoughts, is where everything starts. At this point in transition, it is often difficult to control our emotions, but everyone who is in transition is forced to deal with them. Since your true sense of self is realized inwardly, it's important to understand and accept your internal mindset so your final outcome can be better.

If the unseen is ignored, defeat is inevitable.

Stalling emotionally causes us to be psychologically underdeveloped and stuck, and only the discerning eye can recognize that disasters are waiting to happen.

Going through transition and not being able to process it inwardly, creates a sinkhole, dangerously appearing at other times in life.

A book I read 30 years ago addressing this thought was *Ordering Your Private World* by Gordon McDonald. In an opening chapter, McDonald introduced the concept of sinkholes. His example affected me and I haven't forgotten it. I determined to make sure there were no hidden parts of my own character that would come back to jeopardize my future.

Many people have gaping holes in their lives that are potential hazards to survival.

We are conditioned by society to cover up those places and pretend they don't exist, but admitting their reality and intentionally working to fill in those missing places is the key. Sometimes, harmful distances develop in friendships and families when internal transitions are not properly addressed. I've observed that, often, introverted people, who were once open, can trace the beginning of their "shyness" to a hurt, misunderstanding, transition, or change that wasn't correctly processed. Dealing thoroughly with life transitions is the way to progress.

If you have any hope for your life to be productive, then it's necessary to settle your inward struggles. This is the hard work and ugly part of transition.

Our primary focus must be ensuring that everything "underneath" is dealt with.

Putting on a happy face and walking around like everything is okay, when you're dying inside, is not the answer. Let your contentment be produced from a "complete" inward person. It doesn't take long for others to tell if someone is truly content or not.

Outward change

The second dimension of change is a bridge between the first and third. It's the place where attachment is still visible but disconnection is beginning. I call it *the moment of action*. This can be challenging because it requires letting go of a comfortable past and reaching out to an unknown future. Taking action is an overwhelming part of transition and taking "decisive" action demands full commitment that scares us half to death.

Back to the fly-fishing example, the hatch is the time to immediately capitalize on the changes that are occurring, because it will not last long. Stay with me here. When a bug that struggled to emerge from the bottom of the river, under a rock, off a submerged tree limb or sand bar finally makes its way to the surface, something incredible happens. There's a brief span of time when this creature stretches its wings and flaps them furiously to dry them in the breeze as the current carries the insect downstream. After this amazing unfolding, the bug lifts off from the water with loftier ambitions.

I've seen the hatch take place on numerous occasions and learned about a few things that are at work when it's happening:

First, the fish feeding below the surface are eating bugs drifting by or floating along in that rising process. The movement of the water overturns a rock or stick, dislodging the bug. And when the insect reaches the top, it immediately begins its unique transformation from being wet to dry.

Second, and important to note, this is when the insect is the most vulnerable. There's no escape until that transformation is completed and they go from swimmers and floaters to being able to fly. This is when the trout get aggressive and go into attack mode. Sadly, for the insect, there's no returning to the safety of being hidden under a rock.

Transition is like that. It can literally propel a person from a place of comfort, routine, and limitation, to one of new possibilities, opportunities, and heights never dreamed possible. That is why it is so important to continue on the journey, refusing to get stuck. No matter what the risk, it's imperative to complete the process to attain your full potential.

Third, experienced fly fishers recognize when a hatch is taking place. They can also figure out what type of bug is experiencing this change and match it with a similar hand-tied fly, because, of course, the intent is to catch the unsuspecting fish by fooling it into thinking the fly is real. I know this example may be more interesting to some than others, but the point is:

Outward transition is a stage that can't be delayed or taken lightly without suffering lasting pain.

Take the necessary steps of preparation and then move through this phase quickly and fluidly so that things will work in your favor.

No going back

Remember when I talked about the "Elk-hair Cadis" that my guide introduced me to on my first fly-fishing trip? He was matching the hatch that day, even though I had no idea what was going on. It was an expert move on his part, because this stage of transition is exciting and helps the novice fly fisher to be successful.

This dimension represents what is now on the surface and no longer hidden, leaving the person feeling exposed and vulnerable. It started out as internal but it's different now. Now, deeply rooted feelings become visible. It's an awkward and susceptible place and the greatest challenge is dealing with the pull toward detachment.

In most situations, feeding fish rely on the current to control transitions. This takes place both under the water, where the bug is struggling to emerge, and on the surface where the insect is drying its wings before takeoff. It's a time of gathering strength and showing resolve. For the fish, it's a prime moment for ambush.

To an experienced observer, a person's actions, demeanor, and conversations during this time make his state obvious. And for the one who's going through the transition, it's an enormous challenge because, taking the visible step in owning transition means there's no going back! Under the surface represents feelings that are hidden, but once they're expressed, they're in the open.

It's human nature to ferociously hold onto what used to be while gathering courage to take the next leap of faith. Honestly, it is an uncomfortable and unappealing place. When you see a person facing this reality you notice their vulnerability both in their statements and their actions. Your best response is to offer encouragement and stand with them while the process plays out.

Match your inward and outward selves

Visibility is observing habits and tendencies that are no longer hidden. A verse found in the New Testament says, *"When I was a child, I spake as a child, I understood as a child, I thought as a child: but when I became a man, I put away childish things"* (I Corinthians 13:11). It's key to match our speech and lifestyle. We can't talk like we're in a higher place but actually be living at a lower level. This takes time and an extreme amount of intentional effort to accomplish.

Mark Twain quipped, "Actions speak louder than words, but not nearly as often." In a humorous way, he reminds us that we should reveal externally what we possess inwardly. This is huge for creatures of habit. If something has changed inside, find a way to get the outward to match up with that shift. And try to do it quickly because this outward transitional place of waiting yet working can be difficult if it takes too long.

Most transitional failures happen at this stage. We're in the middle of the dramatic change of emerging emotions, trying to negotiate a new way of actively living, and we find ourselves stumbling, delaying, or getting carried away in the current of unreasonable expectations. The sad result is that so much effort is spent on survival without achieving the goal. It's like instinctively treading water, obsessively searching for a rock to hide under, instead of just spreading our wings to fly. We don't want to become another statistic of loss.

Everybody wants to be a butterfly, but most don't want to go through the cocoon or middle stage of transformation.

Am I not right about this? A butterfly starts out as an ugly worm, eventually attaches itself to a branch, intentionally wraps up in a shroud called a cocoon and finally emerges a beautiful creature everyone adores.

Butterfly bug boards were always more popular at school than the ugly insect ones we already talked about. Isn't it interesting that in the initial and middle stages of transition, these insects are always scary-looking? Those stages are not appealing at all and the last stage always overshadows the others with its beauty. Why are some parts of the process ugly but the last step beautiful? We'll talk about that next.

***

Action Step #8: The next time a friend or family member is having difficulty with a transition, be with him or her and offer a listening ear and words of encouragement.

7. The Other Side of Transitions

Transition brings with it the possibility of something beautiful and unrealized on the other side of the struggle.

The third and final comparison from aquatic life is the bug flying away into a purposed destiny, finalizing the transition. It's the designation of "above" and "overarching."

Discovering individual purpose, what you were created for, is ultimately what transitional accomplishment is all about.

This is the stage where everything comes together. I enjoy thinking and talking about destiny the most. It's what I thrive on. Helping others discover their individual destiny never gets old. But for those moving in that direction, it doesn't come without struggle, forethought, planning, determination, and intense desire. Words like: atmosphere, big picture, greater definition, and defining purpose are all terms that speak to this dimension.

What's happening above?

Something eye-opening for me was the potential happening "above" in the tree limbs shadowing the water's edge. At any given time, there's a plethora of insects on branches hiding among the leaves. They are traversing the tree, feeding, spinning webs, and, basically, doing what bugs do —surviving.

Diehard fly fishermen will tell you that it's possible to catch fish in all three stages but enjoying success in the last dimension may require an outside force like a change of weather. It's interesting when the weather goes south, unlike with fair skies. As the wind picks up and the rain falls, it dislodges some of those creatures from their natural habitat and they fall into the water below.

As you can imagine, this creates a Lancaster County, Pennsylvania smorgasbord for the fish under the surface, anxiously awaiting a meal. It's really fun to tie a fly on your line that looks like a green inchworm or black spider and floating it under some branches during or immediately after a gentle summer rain. The joy and excitement of that type of fishing gets in your blood and makes you want to quit writing and go fishing!

Walk through the door

Just like the fishing guide introducing me to the transitional world of an aquatic bug's life, many people will never find their purpose without help from an outside source. I couldn't have figured out which steps to take, in order to catch that specific species of fish without a clear view and understanding of the new world in front of me.

Although I've written a lot about it, this book is not about fishing. It's a guide to help you successfully navigate change.

You're not an accident, an afterthought, or a mistake. You're valuable, needed, and you possess unlimited potential. Everyone needs a hand to help lift thoughts of expectation to a higher place. Transition brings with it the possibility of something beautiful and unrealized on the other side of the struggle.

Personal discovery is a door into the unfamiliar, but more complete individual.

Alexander Graham Bell said, "When one door closes, another opens; but we often look so long and so regretfully upon the closed door that we do not see the one which has opened for us." This is probably truest when considering transition.

Adventures await those who take that uncomfortable step into the unknown.

A takeaway from the "closing door, opening door" scenario is that no one can force you to leave the comfort of familiarity. You have to decide what to do. When a door closes and you choose to not go through the alternate door, you will find yourself living an unfulfilled life. Don't be content to exist in that type of reality.

I'm walking right now in new dimensions because the closed doors of my past didn't have the power to keep me from walking through the open doors of possibility.

The amazing discoveries that come during times of transition reveal character, growth, and maturity that cannot be acquired any other way. It's natural to think you know who you are and what you're made of when things are uneventful, but times of transition bring out the real you. Life, experienced vicariously through someone else, isn't meaningful. And to a great extent, you will travel the road of life, with all its ups and downs, alone.

In spite of the questions, uncertainties, and doubts, there are new worlds to be discovered that can only happen when you leap into the unknown.

You can gain strength to make your next move by observing others and by looking back on your own accomplishments. Tomorrow will be more rewarding than today if you remember that the last big risk didn't destroy you; it actually brought you to this season. Take advantage of that truth and act without hesitation.

John said about God in the apocalyptic book, Revelation, "*He that openeth, and no man shutteth; and shutteth, and no man openeth… I have set before thee an open door, and no man can shut it*" (Rev. 3:7-8). If you choose to operate on Heaven's terms, there's a finality attached to the workings of God.

He opens and closes doors that only the spiritually-sensitive person can perceive. You may or may not ascribe to these beliefs. However, wouldn't you still agree that there's a part of you that can't be described outside of a spiritual "unknown"? It's true that some of the things that transpire in our lives are unexplainable but evident.

Instead of living frustrated about things you can't change or simply don't have the desire to tackle, why not take advantage of those things that are in your power and leave the other things alone? The truth is, some challenges are going to be the way they are with or without your involvement.

***

Action Step #9: Are you between a closed door and an open door? What you do next could make a huge difference in your future.

Don't forget to download my **FREE PDF: "41 Action Steps to Prepare for and Get Through Transition."**

http://transitionbook.info

Section II—Personal: Navigating Life

8. Life Without a Plan

If you choose to go with the flow of human existence without deliberate individual action, then you will continually suffer unnecessary difficulty.

Everyone has been exposed, in one way or another, to the first step of being successful in navigating life's transitions—planning.

It is virtually impossible to accomplish anything of significance, arriving at your desired location in life, without some type of a plan. Benjamin Franklin stated, "If you fail to plan, you are planning to fail!" Without a workable, achievable plan, failure during transitions tends to be the sad outcome. It doesn't have to be this way and I believe you can succeed.

All kinds of valuable information is currently being offered in the area of productive planning. If you're like me, your email inbox is flooded daily with potential trainings on "how to start a successful business" or "how to master every computer program available" and always, of course, "in five easy steps!" But we know that a plan that isn't doable isn't a reality at all. It's only a recipe for a letdown.

Make a plan that fits you, not someone else

The first step to effective planning is to lay out a plan that fits your personal mindset, skill set, passion, and work ethic.

From our earliest moments of life, others' plans were imposed on us and we didn't know it. It's just the way we are raised and the way we're accustomed to raising our own children. An infant's life begins with few demands outside of being fed, changed, and afforded uninterrupted sleep, although it seems like a lot more to the individuals fielding the ongoing demands! But childcare stripped down is rather basic.

Newborns, toddlers, and young children live the plans of other people—with or without the little one's approval. Parents, family members, guardians, and babysitters all share in the responsibilities of waking the child up, putting the child to sleep, feeding, changing, entertaining, and whatever else the caretaker desires. The baby is living in the adult's world and living by the adult's plans. Those activities become models affecting the subconscious.

A few years later, children are placed in an educational system that decides entry ages, class sizes, hours of attendance, what will be taught, and how many months each year this will take place. The students don't get to choose the frequency of the breaks or the length of time needed to graduate from the process. It's everyone else's plans, not theirs. If it were up to the children, they would allow more time for lunch, recess, summer, fall, winter, and spring break. The entire educational process would be reduced from 12 years down to just a few. And without question, some subjects would be left out, because they don't translate well into everyday life.

Then, in the midst of all the academics, children are introduced to activities like sports, hobbies, music lessons, and a plethora of other things that they don't get to personally plan either. What is now negotiated by the parents and coaches, is practice and performance times, for how long, with which people, and how many times per week. The coaches and parents instruct the children to "do their best" by watching certain people, emulating specific techniques, and pushing past their boredom, lack of interest, pain, sickness, and other issues.

In *Outliers,* prolific author Malcolm Gladwell addressed what is required to become an expert at something. Gladwell said it takes a minimum of 10,000 hours of practice, effort, and focus to become a virtuoso. That 10,000-hour rule has subsequently faced debate. In a *Business Insider* article, Malcolm explained, "There's a lot of confusion about the 10,000 rule that I talk about in *Outliers.* It doesn't apply to sports. And practice isn't a SUFFICIENT condition for success. I could play chess for 100 years and I'll never be a grandmaster. The point is simply that natural ability requires a huge investment of time in order to be made manifest. Unfortunately, sometimes complex ideas get oversimplified in translation."

10,000 hours may sound like an unreasonable amount of time, but I have observed parents, coaches, and teachers driving children, students, and protégés to this type of commitment. Unfortunately, putting excessive amounts of time into any endeavor doesn't guarantee an equal outcome—especially if the plan of others is the main motivation. Those individuals seldom succeed, if they're living a life they have no personal passion for. The best scenario is for a child to have the liberty to choose his own pursuits, strengthened by the encouragement of others, but that type of liberty doesn't often come in the road of life until several more miles have been traveled.

In addition to the previous examples, kids also are expected to go along with the travel plans of their parents. As a kid, I remember thinking my older sister was crazy for not going with the family on vacation one year. I'm pretty sure my parents didn't ask her if those particular dates would work with her teenage "love interest" at the time and she missed out on a fun trip out of the country, that I, as the younger brother, had to go on. She was at an age where she could make that kind of decision. Then, I lived out the same thing myself later when a basketball tournament held more of my attention than a family trip. Are you getting the picture here? Whether good or bad, there are times your life is shaped around the plans of others. When you're young, your own desires and opinions are overridden by the plans other people have for you, but later, as an adult, it's important to carefully consider the path you will take so you're not forced, like a child is, into silent acceptance of someone else's plans.

Those who accept challenging moments, intentionally deciding the road their lives will take, end up with rewarding tomorrows.

***

Action Step #10: Know yourself.

9. To Thine Own Self Be True

Success comes from a series of mistakes that finally turn out right because you kept trying, learning, adjusting, and didn't give up in the process.

One of the first stressors in a young adult's life occurs when they decide to stand up for themselves and make their own plans. It doesn't matter that pressure is coming from parents, school, sports teams, or friends. At some point, everyone decides to either give in to others' plans or move into a place mentally where they make their own.

Here's the truth: you will experience enormous tension when you start making your own decisions. Don't be surprised by uncomfortable trials. Expect them. You're not the first person to be confronted by struggle and you won't be the last—and actually, it should be encouraging to realize that the transition is a natural part of life that will lead you to fulfillment if you navigate it successfully. Don't fall for the belief that, because you're "unique" and have a few meaningful experiences under your belt, it will be different for you. That's simply not true.

The truth is, there's no easy way to gain independence. Personally, I had more than a few moments when I had a huge hole in my heart and a sick feeling in the pit of my stomach because of a hard choice I had to make in order to grow.

Making mistakes until you get it right

Learning to stand on your own feet comes by making right decisions and by overcoming mistakes. You can't have one without the other. Here's the advice I've given my daughters: Success comes from a series of mistakes that finally turn out right because you kept trying, learning, adjusting, and didn't give up in the process.

Nobody gets this right the first, second, third, or hundredth time. There's no magical number or amount of knowledge acquired that automatically produces success. It comes down to an unwavering resolve and determination to survive the trial and error.

Don't start feeling hopeless! Remember that life can turn in your favor at any moment. Who knows? You may be just one decision away from your greatest joy. **Learning the lessons that accompany every new experience prepares you for what's coming next.**

I've learned to give sincere and strategic forethought to the different possibilities and outcomes, and then, even when nothing makes sense, it's possible to live a full life, without being sidetracked or sidelined by change. Take your stand. Be good with where you are mentally and emotionally. Know that those in your life who may not be happy with your plans will get used to the new arrangement. If not, they didn't care as much about you as you thought they did. Of course, I'm not suggesting that every transition will work out right every time, if you just do what you want and ignore all outside input. That would be a massive mistake. Always get wise counsel before you proceed and then remember that some people in your life will be okay with you becoming the truest version of yourself, while others will always be unhappy because you're not who they want you to be.

William Shakespeare wrote in Hamlet, "To thine own self be true." No one goes through life pleasing everyone. But neither do you want to be perpetually opposite of everyone's expectations, just for the sake of being different. Trouble and hardship are present in both a resistant and an acquiescent lifestyle.

If you try to please everyone, you will end up pleasing no one, including yourself. What a miserable existence! Sadly, many people are caught in that trap.

***

Action Step #11: Write down some lessons you have learned from past mistakes.

10. Proactive vs. Reactive

Without a clear perspective and healthy personal ownership of the immediate, it is impossible to possess the future with certainty.

Perception is a vital key to understanding the transition you're facing. How you see, sense, and handle the experience makes a big difference. Here are a couple of questions to consider: What change is coming next? What preparations am I making to get through it successfully?

A mature person is seldom caught off guard because they've lived long enough to know how life works. And they've learned that being proactive is better than being reactive—especially when working through transition. The mature person considers the circumstances before they happen, and then makes preparations to be able to act appropriately. Zig Ziglar said, "Success occurs when preparation meets opportunity."

When there's no forethought and no plan for success, the only possible reaction to an unexpected transition is "flying by the seat-of-your-pants" or "off-the-cuff." That spontaneous, adrenalin-filled response, without a forethought or a secured plan for success, can cause additional stress and misery, not to mention an inevitable crash or a possible detrimental addiction.

Martial artists develop countermoves to defend against surprise attacks. They practice that effective defense until it's automatic. In the same way, when we're faced with unfortunate changes in plans, we don't experience the same stress or anxiety we would have, if we hadn't developed countermoves in advance. When you plan ahead for those contingencies and think through the options, you can then move forward with confidence and purpose.

It's beneficial to understand the importance of living not just in the moment but also to anticipate the next phase of your life. It can be a struggle to find the right balance because spending all your time planning for every possible difficulty is as bad as drifting through life with no thought of your today. Best-selling author Mark Batterson wrote, "One of the biggest mistakes we can make is focusing all of our energy on the next season of life instead of enjoying the season we're in."

Transition is inevitable

Since some things about life are never going to change, we should just accept them. People grow from adolescence to adulthood. Many single people commit to marriage. Actually, in America, estimates show that 80% to 90% of people marry by age 40. All those people move from transition to transition, going from the minor responsibility of being single to committed companionship and then to family obligations. With each of these transitions, there are new pressures and opportunities to be navigated. It's important to be prepared to get through each of those seasons successfully.

Planning and preparing for the future does not mean that you should disconnect from your present responsibilities. **Actually, living purposefully in the now is the only way to effectively navigate successfully through the coming changes.** Without a clear perspective and healthy personal ownership of your current realities, it is impossible for you to take ownership of the future with confidence.

***

Action Step #12: Prepare for a coming change by reading books, talking to friends, and gaining insight about that specific transition.

Action Step #13: As you go through a transition, give full attention to what is happening now.

11. How Will You Handle Transition?

A big culprit to a successful transition process is a nonchalant, "whatever" attitude!

Have you ever been knocked off your feet and completely surprised by what happened? I have. As a kid, I remember standing in knee-deep water at the beach, with no idea of the danger present and I unsuspectingly experienced the power of an undertow.

Intrigued by the rolling surf, I waded in and, before I knew it, the waves had knocked me down and overpowered me. I was immediately pulled under and dragged out to deeper water. Honestly, I felt helpless and found it impossible to reach the surface to catch my breath.

While trapped in this life-threating event, out of nowhere, a hand lifted me to safety. I didn't know the stranger responsible for my rescue, but he was standing close by and saw the whole thing unfold. I'm glad he was there or I would not be here today. That is one of the few times I've thought I might die if I didn't get help quickly.

I'd had no idea that I was so close to danger! Thankfully that man gave me advice about what to look for, how to stand, and how to respond if it ever happened again. I haven't forgotten that near-death experience or the wise words he spoke to me that day.

Like the water that day, life can be difficult, especially if you don't know what to expect or how to resist its undertow. Take what you are reading to heart. I hope you'll learn from my experiences so things can work out for you in a beneficial way.

Prepare for transition! If you don't, the surf of life will knock you down time and time again.

In all likelihood, there's a potentially destructive wave coming toward you right now, so get positioned mentally, emotionally, and physically. Accept the natural rhythm and flow of life, stop fighting it and equip yourself for the process. You never know, you could actually start enjoying the journey!

That day, after almost drowning, I learned three reasons that struggling against the pull of the current is a sure way to drown: One, you will tire quickly, two, you will run out of breath before you get to safety and three, your muscles will seize. And with life transitions, the most helpful action is going back to your preplanned mindset and anticipating the coming split-second to break free. The opportunity will come, no matter how difficult the challenge.

Change is going to come

This is where well-meaning people get sidetracked. You cannot live as though everything will always be the same and nothing will ever change. No matter what you've already survived or what you are currently facing, other transitions will come. They might even show up at the same time.

My wife and I have aging parents in their seventh and eighth decades of life who are definitely dealing with transitions they have never faced before. All four of them are facing many new realities. The changes never stop. And I don't think they will. We've been learning that it's important to prepare and make decisions in advance instead of trying to resolve things while in the middle of a dilemma.

The truth is, you can't trust reactionary decisions as much as you can proactive ones that you've thought through beforehand, when various options are available. Be proactive about living a better life. Don't wait! Put some helpful practices in place today that will strengthen your tomorrows no matter what transitions you face.

Not nonchalant!

A big culprit to a successful transition process is a nonchalant, "whatever" attitude!

Years ago, I had a friend who gave the same answer to every question. He was indecisive, easy-going, and always in a state of "whatever." While that attitude wasn't unusual for a young person, it didn't translate well when it was time to grow up. Holding on to that type of philosophy potentially derails any possibility of becoming the person you were meant to be.

There's no way to know what would have resulted in my friend's life had he moved from "whatever" to actually caring about something. A "whatever" attitude leaves someone like him open to being taken advantage of, run over by everyone else's demands, and not given the chance to live out his dreams.

Because that friendship didn't follow us through the years, I don't know what his adulthood has been like. I'm hopeful that his position changed, and he settled on positive ground so his life could be fulfilling. Most of us learn that there's a time and place to just flow and not rock the boat, but working through a transition isn't the right time.

Being purposely perceptive

It's important to prepare for the future and its possibilities. Some people call it premonition or sensitivity and I believe in the accuracy of those feelings, but I also believe in just having common sense.

Common sense isn't scientific; it's actually a reality that comes as a result of being purposefully perceptive.

Seeing something is one thing, sensing it is something quite different. You might not even be thinking specifically about the transition and you begin to feel uneasy and anxious. Or it's something in the "air" you begin to notice when talking to a friend. A text arrives that reads and sounds a little different. A business meeting hits an impasse that, in times past would not have been an issue. Or an innocent conversation suddenly takes an unfamiliar path. The list is endless. If you've ever had one of those red flag moments, you know exactly what I'm talking about.

Productively handling transition is more important than understanding it

We don't always understand why changes come. Sometimes, in some situations, we find out afterward what the season was all about, however, don't stay in place trying to figure it out because you need to be prepared for your next transition. Who knows? The next bold step might be the one that does make sense.

Be sure not to get caught up in the what-ifs of transitions. It's not necessary to fully understand each one. Just focus on getting through them without losing too much of who you are in the experience. Keep moving with purpose in spite of potential stumbling blocks. If you refuse to row when waves are present, you will end up traveling away from, instead of toward, your destiny.

***

Action Step #14: Draw a simple roadmap of your life.

Action Step #15: If you're in the midst of a transition, take stock of your resources to get through it.

Action Step #16: Brace yourself physically, mentally, and emotionally for transitional waves.

AUTHOR'S NOTE:

Two books that helped me handle transition in my own life are: *The Rhythm of Life* by Richard Exley and *Halftime* by Bob Buford. Both of these aided me in addressing long-term success and significance.

12. Some People Refuse to Move

"I refuse to get lost or sidetracked in my present or future transitions."

Okay, this brings me to the next big truth concerning transition: **instead of progressing, some people get stuck in a particular season of life**. Life transitions are an unavoidable fact of human existence. Knowing transitions are approaching should ignite a fire in you to learn, internalize, and work to get them right. It's my passion to help you get through your life's transitions successfully and a key concept I hope you will grasp is to continue to progress through each season of your life; don't get trapped in the same old situations.

Don't get stuck!

The number one reason people don't make it past certain seasons of transition is they get stuck by refusing to act. They endlessly repeat the hard times over and over instead of working through them. How many friends and family members can you think of who are prime examples of this scenario? They're continuously struggling with the same issue that others have already moved past. I can think of more than a few! Instead of being stuck by the transition, you should strive for perpetual movement forward.

Watch your watch

Are you familiar with the different movements or "caliber" of watches? Here's a short lesson: Watches vary greatly and the main difference is found in each watch's primary power source. A trained eye and ear can easily recognize this by the action and sound of the second hand. Some timepieces are activated by a battery and rely totally on that energy. This design is called Quartz Movement. The second hand continuously starts and stops and it makes a ticking sound. If you glance at your watch, or listen to it, you can tell if that's the type you have. The other type uses what's known as the Mechanical Movement which is powered from both the activity of your wrist and from winding the timepiece. This style produces a fluid type of movement that you can distinguish from how the second hand travels without starting and stopping. Not only is its movement smooth, it's also silent; it doesn't tick.

When a Quartz watch runs out of power it stops and time is lost until the power source is replaced. I've experienced this many times, sending a watch off to the maker or stopping by a jewelry store to get a new battery. But the Mechanical watch is different. It simply requires that I reset the time, wind it, and put it back on my wrist so the movement will keep it powered. An optional way to keep it going and producing accurate time when it's not being worn is to purchase a watch winder that moves periodically in order to keep it wound while in storage.

Like watches, running out of energy to move forward is the discouraging place people often find themselves when experiencing a transition. But living there is even more devastating. People who are constantly starting and stopping tend to lose energy rather than continually and fluidly moving forward. **Structure your life to be constantly in a posture of progression and positive movement.** This doesn't mean existing in a whirlwind of work or busyness, but in always embracing what's next.

Choose to get beyond stuck! Decide that you will never be hung up in the same energy draining spot again. Don't be consumed with dread, confusion, or the nagging thought of giving up. Even though your journey will be different than another person's, determine to keep progressing and refuse to be stopped along the way. One way to do that is to intentionally find something to focus on that will benefit you in another season and pour your energy into that. In other words, work your way through it.

No excuses!

When you look at the matrix of your life are you satisfied with what you've consistently produced? If not, do something about it immediately. You don't want to be that person people shake their heads about and say will never change. Do you really have to learn the hard way every time?

In my sophomore year of college, my friend Jim told me, "The road to Hell is paved with good intentions." That statement challenged me. I accepted the critique and refused to live one more day based on intentions. As a result of that conversation, I immediately began to add positive action into my life. Thanks, Jim, you helped me. I'm happy to still call you "friend."

Public speaker and author Vance Havner said, "Many people are in a rut and a rut is nothing but a grave—with both ends kicked out." People who are always stuck in the same place or find themselves continually getting caught in the same unchanging seasons, are "already dead and don't know it."

The wise writer of Ecclesiastes said, "*Whatsoever thy hand findeth to do, do it with all thy might; for there is no work, nor device, nor knowledge, nor wisdom, in the grave, whither thou goest*" (Ecc. 9:10). Don't be satisfied to exist as you are, in an early grave of your making with no lasting potential. That final transition day will come soon enough without you hurrying it along.

Live your life to the fullest and squeeze every drop of personal possibility out of it. Not only will that advance you but it will also exponentially assist others coming along behind you. Just like me getting tossed around, trapped in a riptide, and dangerously stuck in my life-or-death dilemma, some people find themselves facing the same type of impossibilities. It's true that transition times can be extremely difficult, but there is a productive way through them. Thankfully, in my case, I had a bystander who was observing my near-death experience and stepped in to rescue me.

That, in essence, is what this book is about. You may feel that the difficulty you're going through will never end and could actually be your demise, but there's help! I'm reaching out to pull you up to a safe place. If you find yourself refusing to deliberately act the next time a transition comes, you will, like I did, in that undertow, repeat the struggle without a beneficial outcome. Since that scary life-changing day, I have never entered the ocean again without taking necessary precautions, including being fully aware of what is going on below, on, and above the beautiful blue water in front of me.

Time to grow up

Studies show that people's attention span is decreasing. Advertising researchers Herbert E. Krugman and Thomas Smith found that people need to hear and see the same thing repeated from three to twenty times before they finally internalize the information. Only then will the individual act.

How often do you have to repeat the same transition before you finally learn from it? Unfortunately, the outcomes are the same each time. Instead of things getting better and you being able to move on, you're forced to deal with more hurt, confusion, and discouragement—not to mention the fact that you're no further down the road of life but still trapped in yesterday.

Certain types of unhealthy people tend to be the ones who get stuck and can't move on:

- People who live with the mindset that life is all about them and everyone else exists to serve them, meet their demands, expectations, and desires.

- People who live as consumers and not a contributors. Of course it's okay to act in both roles occasionally, but the healthy disposition should be about adding to every situation and not taking from it.

I've seen grown men and women act like young children; pouting, throwing temper-tantrums, being rude, uncompassionate, and living a self-absorbed life. Those are the types of people I refuse to associate with. They need to grow up. Just because they've experienced some terrible life circumstances gives them no right to act obnoxiously. Many people have lived through horrible situations and have maintained a positive, healthy outlook, but as long as these childish people are content to remain stuck in that same place, they, and the people around them, will be miserable.

Does that sound like you? If you're not getting better and moving on with your life, don't expect to be able to encourage others who are looking for an example to rise above their struggle.

Serve others; find joy

Some of my most memorable moments of joy came when I went out of my way to help someone else. Helping those who can't help themselves truly helps you find healing from your own struggles. John Donne said, "No man is an island, entire of itself; every man is a piece of the continent." You are a part of a larger family, intricately connected on many levels, so choosing to intentionally help others work through their pain will provide you with both mental and emotional strength.

You know well how hard the struggle has been for you? Then, do something to help the next person so they won't have to experience the same turmoil. The best way to keep other people from suffering through the storms you've encountered is to make it a point to recover, be proactive, get up, and get healthy. Then you can share your victories with them. That will give you something to live for; something to look forward to. You can be a difference maker! And you'll be making a difference for your own family.

Many times, I've thought about my own personal challenges and deliberately determined, "I have to do something about this right now, so my children will not be forced to encounter the same thing. I must win this battle so I can pass on the information, strategy, and success to those who mean the most to me. My family needs me to successfully navigate this transition." That thought process made me more determined to do it well.

Decide today to stop being an obnoxious, whiny, self-centered jerk. Instead, look for a way to contribute to the overall success of everyone in your sphere of influence. Be the best example of you that you can be. Do it for your own benefit, but more importantly, do it for someone else's.

***

Action Step #17: If you're stuck in a rut, use the tools in this book—or call a tow truck, (a professional counselor).

Action Step #18: Say this out loud: "I refuse to get sidetracked in my present or future transitions!"

Action Step #19: Write your bucket list.

Action Step #20: Keep a log of what you do every day.

Action Step #21: Volunteer in your community.

13. Destiny Lost

---

*Destiny lost is one of the most heartbreaking things
to watch people experience.*

Serving as a minister for the last three decades has placed me at the bedside of more than my share of people who were close to life's end and eternity's reality. I'm no longer shocked by what matters to people when they're on their deathbed, but sometimes those who are dying are surprised by it. Many feel regrets. In her book *The Top Five Regrets of the Dying*, Bronnie Ware shares an interesting list of regrets from those who are dying:

- I wish I'd had the courage to live a life true to myself, not the life others expected of me.

- I wish I hadn't worked so hard.

- I wish I'd had the courage to express my feelings.

- I wish I had stayed in touch with my friends.

- I wish I had let myself be happier.

Based on these findings, we can summarize that what truly matters is time invested in family, doing the things you love, fostering lifelong friendships, and getting out from under unnecessary pressure. Why not learn from this research and do something about it today? Your life could be drastically changed!

What is your life's purpose?

Everyone has greatness within and a unique reason for their existence that no one else can replace. Unfortunately, some are content to forfeit their ultimate purpose by not reaching towards the achievement they're meant to attain. Personally, I've resolved not to fail in this area. I don't want to look back with any regrets when it comes time to draw my last breath.

A life with purpose identified is a rewarding existence.

One of the most popular self-help books ever written is, ironically, about purpose. *The Purpose Driven Life: What on Earth Am I Here For,* by Rick Warren, has sold tens of millions of copies worldwide and has provided great insight for those who have read it. That subject is the most important discovery of life. Figuring out your own individual purpose will absolutely revolutionize your world.

But purpose alone isn't everything. Destiny is also a major player. And that's a heavy subject that I won't fully address except to say that, everyone wants to know what their destiny is at the beginning of life, but not many are willing to walk purposefully toward it when the destination isn't quite clear. The problem is, there's no way to fully know your destiny without experiencing it. Clarity and development are revealed as you begin moving in the right direction and those who are driven to accomplish their life's purpose will find their destiny on the other side of those achievements.

Of course, you can choose to do nothing and completely miss out on your destiny. Destiny lost is one of the most heartbreaking things to watch people experience. It is contained in your passion or lack thereof.

It's your destiny to help others

Something else that is forfeited by not living out your destiny is the invaluable experience you could offer others. One of the most selfless and interesting acts I've read about in the field of medicine occurred on February 15, 1921. Dr. Evan O'Neill Kane, a chief surgeon performed an appendectomy on himself. He did this because the surgery was needed, because he wanted to know how his patients felt and he wanted to experiment with local anesthesia. Interestingly enough, several years later, he attempted surgery again on himself. This time, it was for a hernia but the outcome wasn't as positive.

Dr. Kane's experiments could be defined as selflessness, craziness, or a little of both. No matter what we think, the truth is, as a result of his actions, lessons were learned and significant procedural changes were made that relieved the pain of untold numbers of patients since then. Learning from our own encounters as well as from the experiences of others, helps life move forward productively.

Your success today, tomorrow, and the next day will not only benefit you but also others who are looking to you as an example.

***

Action Step #22: Meditate on the fact that you're here for a definite purpose. You have a destiny to fulfill.

Don't forget to download my **FREE PDF: "41 Action Steps to Prepare for and Get Through Transition."**

http://transitionbook.info

Section III—Relational Transitions

14. New Worlds Open in Transitional Times

Relational transitions are the most difficult of all transitions.

New worlds open up in transitional times. When you're in the midst of a transition, always look for the lessons to be learned, places to be explored, and experiences to be enjoyed. These new worlds introduce possibilities you've never considered and provide a depth of understanding you've never considered.

Investing in your relationships

The most difficult and, at the same time, rewarding transitions you will ever face are in the area of relationships. Personal, vocational, and spiritual transitions can never compare with relational changes.

Relationship transitions take the highest toll, initiate the most enduring pain, and have the potential to provide life's most rewarding and memorable moments because, when you love deeply, you're susceptible to being fulfilled immensely or hurt deeply. And relationships with their transitions affect us daily which provides us even more opportunities to be challenged. The most notable gains and losses in your lifetime will revolve around relational transitions. Because of this, it's important to get it right.

Healthy relationships demand a total investment. That investment is worthwhile, though because heartfelt commitments result in unimaginable closeness. The problem is that, at the same time, they make you vulnerable to hurt.

Relationships, by their very nature, are always in flux and revolving. Cameron Lee and Jack Balswick revealed in their book *Life in a Glass House* that "most families go through a sequence of stages of development. Each stage begins with an important event in the family's life such as the birth of a baby, a marriage, or a death. The event triggers a time of transition and change as the family adapts to the addition or loss, and the relationships must flex accordingly. This process of adapting to natural changes can be stressful. Thus, it is helpful for families to know the predictable stressors typically experienced at each stage. This has two benefits. First, a family can learn to anticipate and prepare for these changes in advance. Second, when stress occurs, families have the comfort of knowing that, to some extent, the stress is normal for families going through similar changes. Without this confidence, families may add to their problems by misdiagnosing themselves as crazy."

I believe it's imperative to understand this or our families could be negatively affected for generations to come. And it works the same way with all types of committed relationships, whether it's with a companion, sibling, friend, child, or other family member.

Discuss transitions honestly

Lee and Balswick also stated, "Not all families are equally ready to change at every stage. One family may adapt well to having their children enter their teenage years; another family may become rigid and refuse to adapt. This is where a particular family's history comes into play. There are many different reasons for wanting to keep things the way they are. At transitional points in the family's life, the present need for change meets the strengths and weaknesses that have been passed down through the generations. If there's a strong conflict between the two, the family will very likely experience an emotional crisis."

Not only do you, your children, and your friends deal with transitions but your parents do also. It's hard to see your parents growing older and working to deal with all the transitions related to aging. It can be heartbreaking to watch your first heroes trying to own, and be convinced of a new, end-of-life reality. There's a lot to learn—for both generations—and it's always an extremely sensitive subject. If you haven't had those uncomfortable heart-to-heart talks with your parents about living wills and their expectations in the event of catastrophic events, then it's important to gently introduce the subject.

Then there are transitions that are health related, which may or may not be tied specifically to age. Navigating through that minefield is also stressful and taxing for everyone involved—especially if you have to accept that some of those will never change or get better. If you are dealing with the irreversible reality of old age or an incurable sickness, know you're not alone. It's true that those pressures are gut-wrenching, but you can still experience a sense of contentment, and with some courage, knowledge, and determination, you can get through it, and even look back, sometime in the future, with a sense of contentment.

Lee and Balswick's final words on this are, "The essential point is that every family will at some point encounter a change that requires reorganization. How a family reacts depends on its unique history, so no model can be fully universal. But to the extent that the stages are at least common, understanding them can help families have a better grasp of their lives."

In relational transitions, many times, it comes down to holding on, keeping your head above the water, and just doing the best you can. The truth is, you may find yourself in an all-out survival mode, but if you hang on, you'll be able to share your story and help someone else afterwards.

From one traveler to another, I intend to make it through my own future relational transitions just like all the other transitions that have come my way. You can do it too. I believe in you!

In the next few chapters I am going to share about several marriage, parenting, friendship, and death transitions that I have personally experienced. For me, being transparent is the best way I know how to help people. Grab hold of these foundational truths so you'll be prepared when your own transitions come. As you read my real life stories, put a few of the suggestions into practice in your current set of circumstances. You never know, it might help.

***

Action Step #23: If you're going through a transition, find someone you trust who can help support you through it.

15. It's Your Choice

Marriage is, perhaps, the most challenging life transition you will ever face.

Lisa was one month from being twenty and I was twenty-five. She went from a stable home, to the always-changing environment I was operating in, as a full-time traveling evangelist. My job and our marriage forced her to immediately begin adjusting to a completely new dynamic.

You can only imagine her shock as she was thrown into this extremely difficult marriage commitment. I vividly remember her crying every Thursday night the first several months we were married. Why? I didn't know then and only have a vague understanding now. But I repeatedly asked questions like: "Did I do something? Did I not do something? Do you miss home? Do you miss your parents? Can I get you something? Are you sick? What's wrong?" The answer was always the same, no, and it did nothing to satisfy my concern. Lisa and I look back on those days and chalk it up as transition.

Our marriage began like this: After a week away on a honeymoon, we headed off to stay in a pastor's home with no privacy. The only thing we could show them was peace and marital harmony. Evangelizing meant that we constantly found ourselves with other people 15-16 hours a day. Staying in bedrooms with paper-thin walls and using bathrooms with no locks on the doors made life interesting. And that was our life for seven eventful years.

Working on a new marriage without an outlet to say what you think or feel is frustrating! We had to whisper through most of our disagreements and "Come to Jesus" discussions during those first few years. I still laugh out loud when remembering some of those times.

The two shall become one

Marriage is an exciting and eventful type of transition. Going from an independent individual to being responsible for someone else's needs, wants, and wishes requires an enormous paradigm shift in thinking. And it doesn't happen overnight for either party involved.

An adjustment period is unavoidable in marriage. Two completely different individuals with varying values, desires, and expectations are now expected to come together in a combative—no, no, I meant to say collaborative—effort in order become one. "*Therefore, shall a man leave his father and his mother, and shall cleave unto his wife: and they shall be one flesh*" (Gen. 2:24).

Wouldn't it have been helpful if some specific details were included in those ordained words? It would be awesome to have an exact plan laid out to follow that would guarantee marital bliss from day one. Unfortunately, that's not the case. That's why it is necessary to seek advice from wise and successful couples and constantly invest in your marriage. Read books about marriage and go to retreats that deal with enhancing your relationship. Plan date nights. Take romantic vacations. Without a meaningful investment, your marriage will simply flounder.

A transition you choose

Marriage is, perhaps the most challenging life transition you will ever face. The interesting thing, as opposed to many other transitions, is you giddily choose this one. No one forces you in to it, at least not in Western culture. And there's no more important decision to make on your journey as an adult.

Marriage is an act of relinquishing one's self and happily accepting the complete package of someone else's individuality, good or bad. The truth is, you're no longer your own. You belong to each other. That's why this decision should not be made lightly. You should not go into marriage thinking that there's a way out. That only sets up that relationship for potential failure. The sole way for marriage to survive is to approach it with an all-or-nothing attitude. Then the inevitable adjustment period will feel more like a dream and not a nightmare.

In the beginning, when you first move from single and carefree into a committed relationship, you're literally holding on—emotionally—for dear life. The sheer excitement and adventure that comes with this new season makes it fun for a while. Then reality sets in, and the honeymoon needs to be balanced with responsibility on a different level than you have ever known—something that was most likely visible in the home you were raised in, but as a carefree adolescent, you didn't pay much attention to. What a mistake!

Balance is the best way to effectively survive the marriage transition. Honeymoon and responsibility have to exist in the same house! If not, you'll find yourself being pulled toward the ditch of divorce or into the opposite lane of oncoming despair.

The world's first couple is described in the book of Genesis as a finding of one's other self. "*And the Lord God said, it is not good that the man should be alone; I will make him an help meet for him.*" (Gen. 2:18) I love that description. Without Lisa, I am not complete. I'm only half the man I could be. She is my soul mate and we have enjoyed 25 years of marriage to each other.

***

Action Step #24: Play relationship tennis with your spouse or significant other the next time you have a disagreement.

16. The Fun Begins

"Children are a gift to enjoy, equip, and entrust into the guidance of a higher power."

—Drs. Henry Cloud and John Townsend,
Boundaries

The next phase for many couples is KIDS! Childbearing and child rearing requires a brand new learning process. What you weren't "together" on before, you will need to be, when your relationship produces offspring.

With children, you love like you've never loved before and feel the weight of responsibility like no one can explain, and it starts with the first glance at the new life you've produced together.

And then there were three...

I remember the week our oldest daughter, Madison, left for college. I seriously wondered how Lisa and I were going to get through it. Although we began preparing for this moment 18 years earlier and had intentionally ramped up the effort the preceding summer, we found those last few months flying by. Then it was time for her to go, although we got a short reprieve. An Indiana snowstorm, described as a "polar vortex," delayed the inevitable for 3 extra days. In spite of the frigid temperatures and estimated -42 below wind-chill factor, it was a welcomed "natural" event.

To properly express my feelings about her leaving, I'll have to go back to the fall of 1994. At that time, my job had taken us to the Blue Ridge Mountain town of Asheville, North Carolina for a one-night speaking engagement. It was while on this trip that we received the phone call confirming Lisa's pregnancy. We were both excited and introspective. We knew that life was about to change for us once again, and this time, the stakes were much higher.

Anyone with children knows exactly what I'm talking about. To say we were thrilled about being parents would be an understatement. For the first time in my 29 years of life, I was going to be a dad and the thought scared me. I'd never minded pitching in and helping others in the past, as long as it was an option and not a necessity, but this time, the complete responsibility for another person was going to fall directly in our laps.

Not long after we'd gotten the news, I read something that helped me understand my role. As a father, I basically have two primary jobs. One is to protect my children and second is to provide for them. Obviously, different people interpret that responsibility differently, but those two responsibilities are the most important.

A Biblical instruction is found in these wise words, *"Train up a child in the way he should go: and when he is old, he will not depart from it."* (Prov. 22:6) Whatever pattern or principle you, as a parent, choose to follow becomes the benchmark for your children and that training will be with them forever.

Getting ready

We started the process of preparing for the new addition to our family with regular doctor's visits and stocking up on necessary resources like books on parenting and baby names. We also found ourselves intently observing successful parents and asking endless questions of anyone who would give us a few minutes of their time.

Lisa and I also talked about our own unique feelings, ideas, and how these needed to mesh together for us to present a unified front.

Have you ever stopped to consider how much paraphernalia babies need? It is amazing how something so small and unassuming can need so much stuff. Let's make a list, for the fun of it:

Highchair, booster seat, swing, jumper, car seat, carrier, diapers, bottles, breathing machine, nebulizer, medicine, stroller, pacifiers, wet wipes, distilled water, milk, formula, modules, blankets, pillows, crib, basinet, creams, lotions, teethers, etc…

Then there are the amazing things an expectant couple experiences. On a humorous note, Lisa felt great during her first pregnancy; I was the one who got sick! How does that happen?

They grow so fast

That's how it began but not where it ended. Through every phase of the parenting journey, there have been new things to learn. Just when we'd think we had a handle on raising children, they'd moved to another level of maturity, introducing a new set of circumstances.

For instance, don't believe it when you're told the "terrible twos" are an unmanageable time. Actually, the "terrifying threes" are the ones to watch out for. Those 12 months rocked our world. If you've ever parented a daughter, then you're aware of the shock and awe that occurs when she starts affectionately using that gaping hole in the lower center of her sweet little face. Wow, they start talking early and never stop!

I'm smiling as I write, remembering some of those life-changing moments. And your kids grow up fast, so brace for it. They will be up and dressed for the first day of school before you know it. When that emotional day came, I was a grown-up basket case. And in the years following, Lisa and I, along with all three of our girls, always cried and had a morning filled with breakdowns each first day of school. That can be a difficult time for both children and parents.

Disengage for a few seconds of their childhood and it's all over. It's crazy how life will take those babies from our arms of protection so quickly. Then, suddenly, we find ourselves wandering around with our hearts being pulled in all directions. The best you can hope for, after the fact, is that the ongoing influence of your invested time will cause them to stay close to the source of understanding, enduring love, and hope.

It's all worth it

I'm beginning to think there really is something to the proverb, "Blood is thicker than water." One interesting dichotomy I find along these lines is the impossibility of the common statement, "If you love something, then let it go…" I'm not sure if it that's even possible. After trying to apply the principle, I've found, in most instances, it's a futile effort.

Every trek taken in the middle of the night to insure there was no monster hiding in the closet or under the bed was worth it. I don't regret those "one more drink of water and something to eat" moments at bedtime. Lessons, practices, appointments, plays, talent shows, eternal monthly payments for musical instruments abandoned long ago, and a host of other unending events and activities have now passed. Helping develop adolescent friendships, navigating confusing relationships, sorting through grown-up aspirations keeps an engaged parent on their toes and knees.

Then comes the hardest job of all. The most difficult parenting job is the day when you say goodbye and then stand back to see how they turn out. If you made the right investments, their lives should unfold productively. It's hard but you need to trust the process, believing, without second-guessing yourself, that your actions were the right ones, otherwise, you'll drive yourself crazy. The truth is, parenting is on-the-job training, so learn from the information available, prepare for each upcoming transition, and then, just keep doing your best.

People who place a priority on the unequalled privilege of parenting are fully invested in the task. If raising your children in a healthy, cultivating environment isn't at the top of your list, then you're lacking total commitment. What could be more important than helping your children grow up well-balanced?

Saying goodbye

Back to saying good-bye to my firstborn... For days, my chest felt heavy. The only way to describe it is that I honestly wondered if my next breath or heartbeat would come—or if I really even wanted that heartbeat or breath to arrive. I hated feeling that way! I had never been there before and I was miserable.

We had just left our oldest daughter in another state to enjoy her first semester of college. It may not sound like much, but when they are 1,100 miles away, it feels overwhelming. The longest stint of time we had been apart throughout the previous 18 years was just a couple of weeks when she went to South Africa on a mission trip.

My emotions were so close to the surface during that time. A passing thought would prompt a shortness of oxygen, a stinging sensation in my eyes, and a heaviness in my chest. Once again, it's called transition.

Work, plan, and prepare for your children to leave, do it to the best of your ability and wisdom, but take it from someone who has walked down that road, it's still difficult. I was trying to handle it sensibly but wasn't doing well. Until that day, I had never fully understood the underlying dynamics of what happened the day I left home at 19 to embark on my own distant college journey. After helping me load the car and forbidding my mother and sister from showing any tearful emotions, my resolute father broke his own instructions and wept. I now know that feeling.

Cherish the moments

Flying home to Denver with my other two daughters in tow, I could not contain the flood of emotions. I was thinking of how hard it was to let go of one of my precious daughters so she could try her wings and also realizing I would have to face the same thing again with the other two. What this transition with our oldest did was make me want to cherish every moment, not miss one opportunity to exemplify truth, and to give unconditional love to the ones still at home.

In life, you'll come face-to-face with times like this as a young adult, parent, or as both. It doesn't help to resist the inevitable. I've seen people try to hold onto things they should've let go of long ago. Doing this increased their internal turmoil. One example of that is the single mother who discourages her son to date so he can stay home and keep her company. Prolonging the inevitable makes the transition worse and selfishly steals potential from the one with life ahead.

Separation isn't always followed by distance and emptiness. There's actually a joyful satisfaction that comes when the process of trust is completed, and cherished results come afterwards.

In their book *Boundaries*, Drs. Henry Cloud and John Townsend tell us that children are a gift to enjoy, equip, and entrust into the guidance of a higher power to impact the world. My thoughts, prayers, and words about our fledgling college freshman had to take on a new understanding. Isn't it strange what transition will do to us?

During that season, my mind went to a place in the Bible where another parent faced a moment of destiny with her child. The gospel writer John detailed the event this way,

"And the third day there was a marriage in Cana of Galilee; and the mother of Jesus was there: And both Jesus was called, and his disciples, to the marriage. And when they wanted wine, the mother of Jesus saith unto him, They have no wine. Jesus saith unto her, Woman, what have I to do with thee? mine hour is not yet come. His mother saith unto the servants, Whatsoever he saith unto you, do it" (John 2:1-5, KJV)

I know our terminology is somewhat different today, but if I had answered my mother, "Woman, what have I to do with thee," I'm confident that I would have been picking myself up off the floor!

Mary was confident that the investment she had made in this boy (who was now a 30-year-old man) was not in vain. As parents, Lisa and I are raising the girls God has given us, to embrace their place and purpose in life. We should know this, but there are times we forget. Mary believed, as a young expectant woman, that something significant about her son would materialize one day. I don't think she had any idea it would come through her prompting.

Some commentators say that Mary, a unique vessel, had a good feeling about this being the moment that Jesus would embrace his destiny. She was familiar with the inward churning encountered in that moment, since she experienced something similar when an angelic message was delivered to her about an unfathomable conception three decades before. Now, all these years later, the culmination of much excitement, wonder, and expectation was standing right in front of her in the form of a miraculous opportunity.

Don't lose the kids!

Addressed in a separate gospel, Luke revealed an entirely different yet intriguing event.

"And when he was twelve years old, they went up to Jerusalem after the custom of the feast. And when they had fulfilled the days, as they returned, the child Jesus tarried behind in Jerusalem; and Joseph and his mother <u>knew not of it</u>. But they, supposing him to have been in the company, went a day's journey; and they sought him among their kinsfolk and acquaintance. And when they found him not, they turned back again to Jerusalem, <u>seeking him</u>. And it came to pass, that after <u>three days</u> they found him in the temple, sitting in the midst of the doctors, both hearing them, and asking them questions." (Luke 2:42-46, KJV)

Before you think the worst about Jesus' earthly parents, have you ever forgotten or left one of your children somewhere? I have. A few weeks after our third daughter was born, Lisa and I went to one of our favorite lunch hangouts, Veranda in Black Mountain, North Carolina. We were excited about getting out of the house and grabbing a bite to eat. Because of the location of the restaurant, the parking could be dicey. I dropped Lisa off at the front door, drove a couple circles around the busy streets looking for an available spot, and decided to pull around the back of the building and down the hill to a small parking lot.

Quickly, I climbed the stairs, rushed in the back door of the café, knowing it had been several minutes and feeling like I might be holding up the seating process. As soon as I laid eyes of my wife, her look said it all! The BABY? Our newborn was still securely strapped in, right behind the driver's seat of our recently parked SUV.

The panic had to be entertaining to the other patrons as I sprinted back out the door I had just walked through. Our ordeal took a total of 3 minutes; Joseph and Mary's scare was 3 or 4 days. Imagine that!

What kind of craziness must have been going on in the lives of those two and everyone close to them as they frantically searched for the "promised one"? I don't know if there could be any greater stress than realizing that you have misplaced the Messiah. Life can get so hectic that, as parents, we find ourselves susceptible to losing sight, even possession, of the most valuable gifts in our care. A child's physical whereabouts is only one important aspect here. Let this story probe deeper. Where are they in scope of embracing their destiny?

The old public service ad, "Do you know where your children are?" can take on a different meaning. You've been given gifts to nurture and to prepare for future purposeful life participation. How are your kids doing? Do you have regrets? What was Mary to do at the wedding when she faced such a powerful moment of opportunity?

In my estimation, she was resilient given the extreme pressure of the whole running-out-of-wine "faux pas" and the fact that Jesus intended to keep a low profile. Would she freeze, take ownership of her son, circumvent divine appointment, and let selfishness and near-sightedness control her spiritual judgment? Or would this obedient lady make a critical move to set in motion the wheels of ancient prophecy?

It's amazing how powerful a few purposeful words can be. Jesus said, "Not now…it's not my time" and Mary said, "Do whatever He says." Without having the bigger picture in mind, it would be easy to find yourself playing life safe for the sake of feelings, when your children are involved.

The rest is history. Jesus responded to the one person who believed in Him the most and performed the first of many public miracles attributed to His ministry. In turning water to wine, Jesus set a precedent of miraculous transitions that continue even now. He still changes whatever we give Him in faith. What appears to be a setback ends up being a celebration when He touches it. And tough transitions can turn out successfully too.

When it comes to children, transitions are coming and there's nothing any parent or guardian can do to avoid that reality. It never turns out well when this single truth is manipulated to benefit the parent instead of the full development of the child. But Mary wasn't thinking of herself. She was thinking about the comfort of the wedding participants and also about Jesus stepping into His greater purpose.

Here are some questions…What would you have done in Mary's shoes? How have you handled those monumental transitions? How are you doing with it right now? When those transitional times arrive, what are you planning to do?

Jesus responded because of the faith He had in his mother. It's a weak cop-out to place blame elsewhere if things are not where they need to be with your children.

What should you do?

Let's wrap this chapter up by considering a few vital points.

1. If you're a spiritual person, then you know the children under your supervision belong first to God. Right? Taking responsibility to invest your best in them is an absolute, but assuming final ownership is dangerous. Jesus was Mary's miracle baby, but His purpose was bigger than she could contain.

2. A total investment of time, resources, and wisdom is absolutely necessary to complete the task at hand. Approaching this halfheartedly doesn't end well.

3. Unconditional love is the only way to parent a healthy child. When love is measured, emptiness is sure to develop for the parent and confusion for the child.

4. Understanding the many roles a parent must embrace can be overwhelming unless you continually prepare for them.

5. Using less than positive past experiences as excuses will not release you from dealing with the parenting responsibilities constructively.

6. Holding onto what was, will never produce or bring about the potential of tomorrow's destiny. At some point, you need to push the plan forward no matter how heartbreaking it might be and then, in the end, you'll be able to enjoy the brilliant outcome.

It's a privilege to nurture world-changers

The pain of transition does ease over time, but that isn't what you want to hear in the moments of goodbye. Unfortunately, putting a grown child back into her basinet really isn't a viable option so it's necessary, as a parent, to release them when it's time, no matter how hard it is.

Countless times, I heard my mother say, "I don't say goodbye." This is her way of dealing with the frequent departures of people who hold a special place in her life. Thankfully, she has always been geographically situated close to my only sibling Cyndi. Sadly, most of my adult life has been spent hundreds of miles away from her, with only one or two visits home each year. I've made it work for the sake of ministerial calling and when you raise children for life and spiritual fulfillment; it demands that you let go, even though it affects the heart—your body's most vulnerable place and the seat of all emotion.

Cherish, invest, develop, and accept the privilege of nurturing world changers. Time is too precious to get caught up in playing the guilt game. If it's time to let your children go, don't increase the pressure by making it impossible for them. That won't help either of you. Just accept it; life moves on in good times and bad.

A simple word of warning, don't allow lasting misery to take over your life. Work to foster an environment of purposeful change and focus on the joy you received from the privilege of being able to raise a successful child.

And in case you're wondering about the outcome of my struggle in letting our daughter go, the verdict is still out. I actually have two gone now! If you have already walked this road, I commend you, and if, by chance, it's looming large in your future, success is attainable.

***

Action Step #25: If you're a parent, examine your relationship with your children no matter how old they are and ask yourself if you're holding them back in any way.

17. More Fun

---

*I would never try to stop my daughters from taking
the next step toward their personal destiny.*

Recently I experienced another unwelcomed relational transition.
And it happened in a hurry so I didn't have much time to prepare
for it. Thankfully, these types of scenarios don't happen often.

For me, it happened when my middle daughter decided to join her
older sister at college in another state. Was I sad? Yes, but not just
sad; I was devastated. Both her decision to go, and everything
involved in making the move, all happened in just one week's time.
Quick relational changes leave feelings that are raw and exposed.

Drs. Cloud and Townsend wrote about situations like this in their
book, *Boundaries:* "In the practicing phase children learn that
aggressiveness and taking initiative are good. Parents who firmly
and consistently set realistic boundaries with children in this period,
but without spoiling their enthusiasm, help them through the
transition."

The authors were obviously addressing earlier stages in life, but I
believe the principle also holds true in the later years of adolescent
development. For us, with our daughter's sudden decision, we've
found the change hard but manageable, mostly because we believe
she made a good decision for her future that will prove
advantageous in the long run.

Not all separation and relational transitions have to do with death or divorce. Sometimes, as in our case, it's about loading the cars of a twenty-year-old and a seventeen-year-old and saying goodbye, knowing that a lot of life's "purpose" is unfolding in that moment. What's difficult to deal with is the understanding that things will never be the same again, although "things not being the same" doesn't necessarily have to be bad.

Accepting the reality of the transition

The night before they left, I lay awake for hours, trying to accept this transition. I had a strange feeling I hadn't experienced before and couldn't get past. On the one hand, my wife, girls, and I were all under the same roof with everything meaningful in life intact. As a father and husband, everyone I am responsible for was protected, in good health, happy, and secure. That night, there was no wondering about where they were or what was going on in their lives. I felt peacefully content, which was amazing. Isn't that what everyone is striving for, when it comes to your family?

But on the other hand, I was trying to cope with the fact that in just a few short hours it was all going to change. Two of my three were leaving and I was painfully hoping that Lisa and I had gotten this parenting obligation right. One of the main questions rolling over in my mind was about whether we had done everything we could to prepare them for this pursuit. It really was emotionally overwhelming.

I was experiencing that place of transition between the internal feelings of being connected and those first few moments of external disconnect. A flight was taking off and it was stressful for everyone involved, especially the ones living through the reality.

Many times since that night, I've wondered where my daughters were and what was happening with them and when I think of them,

I often find myself fighting both tears and shortness of breath. The feelings are, at times, difficult, crazy, and unbearable.

Don't take this the wrong way, but if I could keep them at home forever, I would, just like some of you! But I raised them to achieve great things, so holding them back now wouldn't be right. Of course, they will always be my babies and I will take care of and defend them with my last ounce of energy, but this is their transition into individual purpose and I would never try to stop them from taking the next step toward their personal destiny.

Letting go

This observation by Lee and Balswick from *Life in a Glass House* resonates with me. They wrote, "Parents should also begin to redefine themselves as something other than adults with dependent children. This is a difficult transition for many on both sides of the generational line. Some parents and children have a very difficult time letting go of each other. Yet they must let go for the healthy differentiation of all concerned."

Our 17-year-old finished high school a year early, which is a huge accomplishment. She took a full load of classes that last year, going in an hour early every morning and staying until after the final dismissal most days. It was a true act of commitment and a display of responsibility. Because of this, Lisa and I felt that she could handle the move to the small, private college, even though she was still two months away from being 18. But it was still hard for me to let her go.

And the decision wasn't easy for her to make either. Her obvious desire to be here to support her little sister and the things we are involved in amazed me. We literally had to convince her that everything would be good and it was okay for her to be young and enjoy this stage of life. I could hear in her words and feel in our interactions those last few days, how difficult this was for her. I love all three of my girls unconditionally and am proud beyond measure of what each one of them is becoming. I realize how blessed I am.

Children have to deal with transitions too

One reason I feel passionate about addressing this particular transition is because of the difficulty our ten-year-old daughter has faced with both of her sisters gone. It has torn my heart out, to see her inundated with sad emotions again and again.

The day the girls left, my youngest and I went to a wedding a couple of hours away. We helped them load their cars that morning, said tearful goodbyes, got a few miles down the road, and had to go back. I went back because, in my haste to depart for the wedding, I had totally forgotten to lay my hands on them and say one last prayer of protection, guidance, and destiny over them. No way was I not going to turn around and do this! Our family is built on faith and total dependence on the One who fills heaven and earth.

When Marley and I returned home later that night, the house was not the same. It was empty, dark, and strangely silent. That's when it hit me like a ton of bricks, although I tried, unsuccessfully, to keep it together for my little one. It didn't take long to realize that she was feeling the same way as me. After going to her bedroom, beside both of her heroes' rooms, she realized immediately everything was drastically different.

I think this was the first time in her ten short years of living that she had to deal with something that heart-wrenching. She was quiet and I knew there was no way I could let her walk through that moment alone. By the way, this is a key to your survival and ongoing emotional balance during transition. **Don't face transition by yourself. Reach out to someone who will walk through it with**

you. And, by all means, afterwards, look for someone in transition who you can help.

When I got to Marley, she was crying because of a sweet note left on her bedroom door. As I pulled her close she said, "Dad, Madison left me a note like the one I left on her door." We cried together as I reassured her of her sister's love and how I knew that this was a hard time for all of us. We chatted and then she ran to get a pillow that her sister had given her. Marley has held onto that pillow and slept with it every night since they left.

I don't want to paint a picture that all is lost or that geographical distance automatically means we're no longer emotionally close. Our family will always be close. This is just another transition that has to be processed correctly. I realize that they're reaching towards their personal advancement, but I do hope that, in time, their destiny will bring them each back into close proximity of home. Okay, I was being diplomatic. I really want them to always be nearby and know that the door of my heart is always open for them. My love for them is never-ending.

I talk candidly and transparently about transitions in my children's lives because there's no way to completely separate my life from theirs. Being a husband and dad are my greatest privileges. Lisa and I have three beautiful daughters and there's no way to fully express the depth of emotions we've felt with each of their births. Of course we've given a lot but we've received so much back as a result. We've learned that there are enormous rewards attached to selflessly handling parental responsibility, and nothing else in life can be compared to the love, fulfillment and appreciation that are reciprocated.

What if the family isn't healthy?

Children are a blessing. They bring a joy unknown without them. But sometimes a child is raised in a home where one or both parents are disengaged. Can the child make it? Can he become an emotionally-sound adult? Absolutely. In fact, I constantly see how resilient people are in spite of the unfortunate circumstances they were dealt as children.

Of course the smoothest family units are those that are intact, where each person understands his or her role, and all are mutually invested, but it's possible for those raised in unhealthy families to rise above unwanted turmoil. This happens through sheer determination and always shows the exceptional quality of that individual. I'm amazed and impressed by people who defy the odds and still accomplish greatness. Truthfully, it's hard to survive even when everything is in order, but those resilient people show that, even if they can't choose the circumstances they start with, they can positively influence their results.

Dealing with a "broken" home

Being accessible for your child through their transitions is what being a supportive parent is about. It's challenging but easier with an intact home. For those who are traveling down the road of divorce, helping your children when your own life is full of upheaval is more difficult. It's important, for your child's sake, to put much of your own life on hold until your parental obligations are fulfilled. Good parents have times where they need to put their own dreams aside until their child makes it through his own transition.

Don't spread yourself too thin!

These concepts can also be applied to other relational connections, such as extended family and friends, but the truth is, your family should be the most important. It's where your energy should go. It's sad to see people put a greater investment in their job or in complete strangers than they do their own family. It's no wonder that some of the most important transitions in their lives haven't ended well.

Everything you invest in takes a part of you. When you juggle too many different passions, it's impossible to accomplish anything very meaningful. Be sure there's enough of you to go around without forfeiting yourself in the process. Give to those who matter most or none of the rest of it will be worth it at the end. And get support yourself! The best support most often comes from your parents, siblings, your spouse or your children. And from my view, complete parents have a better chance at raising complete children.

Goodbye

Goodbye is, perhaps, the hardest word we ever have to say. Having all my girls nearby at home makes me feel happy and complete—unlike when they are four or five states away. During the first few weeks after my two daughters left for college, many friends and family asked how I was doing, and the only answer I could give was, "not very well; I'm just trying to get through this." Someone even reminded me that I was writing a book about transitions while I was facing one at the same time.

I think my next book will be about vacations, happiness, and abundance.

***

Action Step #26: Write down what you will gain from your current transition that you will, one day, rejoice in.

18. Friendship

Hold onto true friends.

In the fall of 2007, I was elected senior pastor of a 41-year-old church in Fayetteville, North Carolina. With that move came enormous challenge, growth, and opportunity. I experienced many bright spots in the months leading up to that move and in the four years that followed.

But, as you can imagine, not everything in a transition of that magnitude is easy. In fact, the 48 months of leading that church included a few of the most difficult days of my life. I was able to navigate through them by constantly reminding myself of my purpose and the divine objective. Thankfully, those brief dark moments were not permanent or lingering.

During that pastorate, Lisa and I formed a connection with a young couple serving in the role of youth pastors. Initially, we didn't realize how valuable that friendship would become, but over time, that friendship grew into something bigger than we expected. Knowing that someone has your back and is fully committed to the direction that you are leading an organization is comforting and reassuring. Of course there were others who were also supportive, but this particular couple's story reveals a type of relational transition that I want to discuss.

Through those years of working together, our connection grew. And when it came time to act on my next vocational move, which would require a 1,700-mile relocation, that committed couple stepped up to make the move with us. It was their sincere desire to take this huge step of faith to work with us and continue the closeness that we had developed. It meant more to our family than words can describe and further solidified our appreciation for them.

There are times in life when you need someone to stand in the gap, be a real friend, and offer unconditional support. This couple provided that for us. But as life would have it, and after working together for three years in the new location, the day came when that friendship, which had stood the test of time, took a transitional turn. Because of their loyal friendship, we will always have a lasting connection with the Nance family that distance cannot diminish.

When they made their next life and career move, which took them to another state, we shed both tears of joy and sadness. I am thankful for the eight years we spent together and for the level of trust and confidentiality that we enjoyed. I wouldn't want to think about what Lisa and I would have done without them during so many difficult and eventful days. By the way, they moved just a few weeks before our two oldest daughters decided to move out of state for college which reminded me that there are times when multiple transitions hit you all at once. To say 2015 was an easy year would be a complete lie. Did I mention relational transitions are hard? If, I haven't, let me say it, RELATIONAL TRANSITIONS ARE THE MOST DIFFICULT OF ALL TRANSITIONS.

Friends are not necessarily friends forever

Not all friendships are beneficial. Can you think of someone who is holding onto an abusive relationship they should have ended long ago, but they will not let it go because of false security? It seems that everyone else can see it's hopeless except for the person who will not come out of that deathtrap.

Some personal connections are poisonous, and the sooner people realize it and take steps to depart, the better off they are. This is especially evident in catastrophic marriages, where moral failure, abuse and outright rejection occur. If you have experienced this or are facing this tragic position, don't just stay there. Get out of that environment for your safety, and reach for something greater in life.

You can also experience adverse feelings in friendships that fall on difficult times. I've had certain connections in the past that I thought would last forever. But I was wrong! Some alliances, that fit your life at a particular time, are not beneficial for your future and they don't survive the tests of time or of unavoidable transitions. This doesn't have to be a bad thing. In fact, the loss of that friend could open up a space in your life that can now be filled by someone who has the knowledge to help you navigate through your next season of change.

When I think about some lost friendships of my past, it's plain to see that I was spared unnecessary damage because those individuals were not capable of supporting me through my life's transitions and would have held me back. Do I wish that some separations had ended differently? Absolutely. But no matter how they happened, they were necessary.

We've all known people who were too demanding. These are the people who are aggressive and insensitive to anyone else's desires but their own. I've observed, many times, devalued individuals succumbing to the aggressor's self-serving plans, often to their own downfall. Those so-called friends can be more harmful than helpful to a person's future when not put in their proper place.

You've probably experienced faulty friendships where you were always fulfilling someone else's expectations, knowing that if a disagreement arises, that friendship will end. So, you acquiesced to their purpose and sacrificed your own desires. Wasn't it freeing when you found out you could survive without that relationship?

There will always be individuals in your life who refuse to support you as you deal with your life's challenges and opportunities. They will always think they know better. The truth is, some of those friendships and alliances must be purposefully left behind if you want to reach your destiny. You have to cut ties with those who are keeping you bound to a cause or mindset that no longer enhances the direction you want to go.

And if you have true friends? Hold on to them! Listen to their advice and take time to weigh it out.

"Where no counsel is, the people fall: but in the multitude of counselors there is safety" (Proverbs 11:14). Those ancient words are still true. Ultimately, if some type of action needs to be taken to get through the transition before you, be certain that it is the correct course of action, based on the counsel of wise friends, along with healthy personal deliberation.

***

Action Step #27: Make a list of your friends—good, bad, and questionable.

Action Step #28: Ask your true friends for advice regarding your plans.

Don't forget to download my **FREE PDF: "41 Action Steps to Prepare for and Get Through Transition."**

http://transitionbook.info

Section IV—Vocational: Personal Alignment

19. You Gotta Start Somewhere

It's important for kids to transition from the "do it for me, I'm special and don't have to work" mindset early in life so they won't miss out on valuable learning opportunities.

A study of the subject of transition would not be complete without looking at vocational transition. Our work is a major part of who we are as people.

My vocational path, outside of chores around the house, began as a young teen with a plethora of menial jobs, but I was fortunate enough to settle into a rewarding career in my early 20s. Here's a "30,000-foot flyover" of how my vocational life has played out. Your journey may contain some similarities with mine.

Learning to work

My first "real" job was cleaning Gerland's grocery store floors late in the night hours between closing and opening. Gerland's was a popular place in the early 1980s with several locations in Houston, Texas where I grew up. A few of my buddies worked there for a family friend who attended our church and taught the youth class. He was "kind" to offer me employment and, now that I look back on it, I'm sure it was a setup to keep an eye on my friends and me.

It's interesting how an opportunity like that can provide a sense of pride and accomplishment, even at a young age. It's important for kids to transition from the "do it for me, I'm special and don't have to work" mindset early in life so they won't miss out on valuable learning opportunities. When talking about a job, I've explained to my children that **work is not only about the money you make or the things you produce. It's more about the confidence, experience, and satisfaction that come with being a contributor not a consumer.**

I learned several important things on that first job, including the importance of:

- Deadlines and time restraints—We had to get the floors done before the store opened, which meant no slacking on the job.

- Following a preplanned schedule—I had to show up when I was supposed to.

- Physical labor—There were no automatic scrubbing and waxing machines available, so we did most of the work by hand (although learning to operate a floor buffing machine was an adventure all its own).

Armed with cloths, brooms, dustpans, and trash cans, we cleaned all the floors, carefully removing the dirt. Next, we filled yellow buckets with water, added cleaning fluid, hauled them around the store, worked with mops and squeegees, wrung out the grime through a contraption connected to the buckets, and emptied the filthy water. Then we switched over to stripping solutions and applied it to the freshly-swept and mopped areas. After that, we had to rinse the containers again and prepare for the wax to go in the same buckets so it could be spread evenly on the floors. This was no cakewalk!

We dealt with set-backs like missing equipment, workers not showing up, and broken wheels on the mop buckets. Once, while trying to use a bucket with a broken wheel, I spilled the bucket of wax twice in one night! And, of course, it happened at the most visible location near the registers, right by the front door, which caused a panic throughout the crew to get my mess cleaned up before opening time. Thankfully, we did get it done with few minutes to spare and I learned in the early hours of that morning not to use a broken piece of equipment. Get it fixed or use something else!

I also found out on another night that Red Man chewing tobacco wasn't for me, but I'll save that story for another time...

Vocational effort is vital

Lessons learned while "on the job" can never be acquired while sitting at home. For most people, the first transitional move toward employment is stressful. And, in many cases, that first job doesn't last long, but it's okay, since you're trying something new that's totally out of your comfort zone. And you're learning that it's not easy to navigate those momentous events in your life. Sometimes it takes everything in us to face the day ahead.

The same thing can be said about vocational transitions. When you're facing a job change, it's important to travel through the process correctly so you can be building a plan for future success. This is huge since you obviously can't move forward or be financially independent without hard work. The following verses speak volumes:

- *"In the sweat of thy face shalt thou eat bread..."* (Genesis 3:19)

- *"...If any would not work, neither should he eat"* (II Thessalonians 3:10).

- *"But if any provide not for his own, and especially for those of his own house, he hath denied the faith, and is worse than an infidel"* (I Timothy 5:8).

Do meaningful work even if you don't "have" to work

For most people, there's no choice but to get up every day and produce. Of course there are a small percentage of people who are born into this world without the demands of work. Even though this "fortunate" class carries the label "privileged," in many cases, the unearned wealth isn't an advantage at all. While they may never have to worry about having a place to live or their next meal, they deal with their own unique struggles and transitions. For some, there's an ongoing negotiation to obtain parental attention and acceptance. Then many of them have an entitlement mindset and they find it impossible to relate to everyday people and life.

It's interesting to hear about wealthy individuals choosing to not leave their children the entire family fortune. One I found remarkable was the decision of Bill Gates of Microsoft fame. He and his wife, Melinda, have given away tremendous amounts of money to charity and do not plan to leave their billions to their children. Gates revealed to a TED conference audience in Vancouver that his intention was to leave each of their three children $10 million from his estimated net worth of $76 billion. The Gates' reasoning has to do with creating, for their children, "a sense that their own work is meaningful and important." He wants them to "have a sense of their own ability." They also had a desire for their children to "remain balanced," which they felt was impossible without, as they put it, "finding their own self-worth."

Can you imagine, if you were one of the three, only getting a measly $10 million? Poor things. The rest of us, who are not so "privileged," have to find our own productive vocational path.

My vocational meanderings

It can be daunting to find your optimal career choice and seldom do people find it early in their working career. Many work in an endless series of one unsatisfying job after another until they find their way. I sure did.

After the grocery store job, I worked as a laborer moving mobile homes and trailers around southeast Texas. What this employment position entailed was: extreme heat, early mornings, late nights, fueling trucks, diesel fumes, mud, dirt, railroad ties, downpours, flashfloods, steering wheels without power steering, tie down machines, sledge hammers, jacks, flat tires, critters, busted fingers, splinters, sheets of plywood, a sore back, aching body parts, and many other exciting things. Sounds fun, doesn't it?

I was relieved to exchange that job for one as a courier for the same company. This amounted to paying bills, dropping off checks, and delivering supplies. What kept this one interesting was that the business was owned by my brother-in-law and sister. Working for family has its own set of transitional lessons—most of which has to do with putting personal feelings aside and staying focused on completing the tasks.

Then I transitioned into a job of working as a cable subcontractor's helper in the early days of that technology. It seemed like everyone wanted access to cable television but houses and neighborhoods were not wired for the advancement. That's where we came in. There was plenty of work to be done and money to be made. I know that "cable subcontractor assistant" sounds better than "ditch-digger," but my responsibility was to dig ditches to bury black coaxial cable from the home to a green cable box located in the back corner of each lot. While everyone else on the crew did the inside installation (the fun stuff), I was getting paid ten dollars a house to do manual labor outside dealing with shovels, picks, sun,

Texas heat, sweat, bugs, shrubbery, rocks, roots, snakes, humidity, undergrowth, and overgrowth.

Finally, a new opportunity came my way: the chance to take as many daily appointments as I could complete. I quickly learned to manage my own schedule and time and found that it was possible to complete about ten jobs before noon. A hundred dollars a morning wasn't bad for a teenager!

My vocational progression during those few years amazes me. Somehow I learned to apply valuable and previously acquired information and skills to each new job. Even though the fields were different, many of the principles worked, no matter what the specific job was. Much of vocational success has to do with adapting things already in your knowledge and experience base to the new expectations presented.

I left the cable field and started working at The Remington, a 5-star hotel, as an automobile detailer. I started the job with the hopes of becoming a valet on the upper drive instead washing cars in the underground garage. Eventually I did work my way up to being a valet on both the hotel and restaurant drive. I won't share the many events that took place on that job, but I did learn a lot from the wrecks, fights, customer service challenges, tips earned, and the furious customers.

I made money on that job while also learning the value of so many aspects of vocational skills, such as: covering someone else's shift, not being cut, going in before 6:00 A.M., staying until midnight and interacting with affluent customers. Eighteen-hour days on your feet will wear on your body and psyche, but, on a side note, in the slow times, I learned how to juggle the wadded up parking tickets.

Book learning too

During those few years of employment transition, I finished high school and did a year of college at North Harris County Junior College. Then, for the next three years, I was in Jackson, Mississippi earning a bachelor's degree. That decision, which took me eight hours away from family and friends, was another eventful transition all of its own.

I went through many vocational changes and, as a result, I developed a personal expectation for financial growth and improvement. I also realized that, for this to happen, it would require additional effort. My thoughts soon shifted from working harder to working smarter and I've used that mindset in many other life pursuits as well.

After college, I spent ten years traveling full time as an evangelist, preaching week after week in different locations. That time on the road required constantly transitioning to different homes, churches, people, cultures, cities, and states. Being introduced to a new normal every few days was taxing on many levels, plus Lisa and I were married three years into that stint. Previously, I had traveled a short time with my college roommate and lifelong friend, Kevin.

I averaged around 220 speaking engagements per year during that decade. That's a lot of services and circumstances to learn from. There's no way to describe the various transitions that needed to be negotiated in order to be successful at that lifestyle. It boiled down to hundreds of thousands of miles traveled by land and air along with the stress of no guaranteed pay amount, dealing with thousands of people in hundreds of churches, and the countless difficulties associated with a constantly fluctuating schedule.

Starting over again and again can get tedious, but it's rewarding if your efforts are directed toward a specific purpose.

***

Action Step #29: Take stock of what you have earned. Can you see the benefits beyond the financial improvements?

20. Taking Risks

Never travel the transition road alone.

The earliest transition memory I have happened when I was 4 years old. Although I was too young to remember the details, I do know it happened as a result of a vocational change. The year was 1969 and my family was relocating from Houston, Texas, where I was born, to Dayton, Ohio. It was an exciting time because my father had just assumed his first pastorate. This was major change for our family since he had never before experienced full-time ministry.

Up to that point, my father had worked in the business world for GMAC. He had only spent a few years exploring ministry opportunities previously, and only when his busy schedule of family, vocation, and Bible college pursuits permitted. The day-by-day events of the 5 years we lived in the Buckeye State escape me now, but there are a few things that have followed me through life.

Early transition

Being away from extended family was something we were forced to deal with; distance is a reality with many vocational transitions. But my sister, parents, and I had each other as well as the first few families who came into the church during that time. They still hold a special place in my heart and memory. And, speaking of memory, I also remember the names of my neighborhood friends from over 40 years ago: Bobby Kellogg and Shawn Kelleher.

Much of what defines my life today can be traced back to those early years of childhood development. Not long ago, I had the privilege of preaching in that city and church. While we were visiting, I enjoyed showing my family a small piece of my history by driving by the elementary school I had attended, as well as the last house we lived in there. Those places seemed to be much larger back then.

Things were different in Ohio than what we were used to in Texas, but many life-shaping events happened while living there. It was amazing to watch my parents invest themselves into building a community-impacting ministry. In those brief years, the church grew from a meager beginning with only twenty people or so, to a congregation of a few hundred people. Lives were forever changed, property acquired, buildings constructed, recordings made, and student trips taken to bless and reach others in "distant" states such as New York and West Virginia. Great memories, but it was a transition nonetheless.

Back to Texas

1974 brought a new transition as we headed back to Houston for a pastorate in a well-known church. The story of this next church wasn't exactly the same because, "it was the big leagues," but there were a few similarities, such as land acquisitions, building projects, and memorable growth. The bright spots were not as abundant for me during that time, but I am thankful for the life lessons and friendships there.

What I learned most, both in Ohio and Texas, was that when purpose demands a drastic move, those with a "true-north" sensitivity will abandoned caution and walk off into the personal unknown in order to fulfill their purpose. I also learned that positive and lasting results can be realized in the best and worst of situations. Something good can come out of the biggest or smallest life and ministry opportunities as long as you remain consistent and diligent through every circumstance.

Those two geographical moves meant new homes, schools, playgrounds, friends, cultures, cities, surroundings, weather, and mindsets. Embracing the new and letting go of the old required both inward and outward transition.

Choosing a transition

Isn't it interesting how many times you end up as an adult living out what was modeled before you as a child? You can't guarantee that it'll happen for those coming after you, but you can strengthen the lessons through faithfulness to the process. There's no way to calculate exactly what is being impressed upon young minds in their formative stages, but it will be revealed over time. Here's how that truth happened for me:

May of 1987 had finally arrived and I was graduating. College was over and the next chapter of vocational life was beginning. Just as with my high school graduation, my close college friendships were losing their tight bonds at the hands of transition again. We were going in many different directions with anxious hopes for great accomplishments in our new ministries.

For me, the excitement of the road as a traveling evangelist was calling. Some may wonder how a 22 year-old could be so confident about deciding to embark on this adventure with no promise of survival. In my case, that decision was directly tied to what I had observed through my parents. It was also because I did not want to walk the safe, well-worn path of job security. I wanted to step out by faith and see what God would do.

Taking a step of faith demands a continuing life of faith. Don't miss the significance of that statement. Ministry is a people-based business, and people are fickle. There's nothing like not knowing where the next stop, meal, bed, and meeting will be. Because I realized that, I really wanted to have some type of assurance about this ministry choice, before graduation. The confirmation came from much soul searching and after declining other employment opportunities. Needing a sign that, "Yes, this is right, do it" was the foremost thought on my mind during the last few months of school. And I was thankful that I did get the affirmation on a Sunday evening through a peer, Scott, who remains a close friend, all these years later.

Full time ministry

The following ten years of travel brought many great memories and a wealth of invaluable experiences. During that time, I ministered in a host of churches throughout the United States and internationally, speaking an average of four to five times a week. All that traveling opened my eyes to much that was positive and negative, all at the same time.

If you've experienced it, then you know the obvious differences between being a welcomed guest and being just a visitor. A guest is someone who is prepared for; a visitor is one who just drops by unexpectedly. Full-time travel lets a person know exactly how the host views them.

It's also easy to tell whether or not the individual in charge has experienced life outside of their safe and familiar surroundings or not. Their hospitality, preparedness, and attention to detail all speak volumes. For the itinerate minister, it's imperative that he or she learns to adjust, flow, and become familiar with the many transitions presented by life on the road.

I found that it was important to maintain at least a minimal schedule and routine so that each new week was as free from frustration as possible. I also worked to stay centered on the primary purpose for my calling, since eternal endeavor is of utmost importance.

Traveling the transitions together

With every transition, there are treasures to discover and embrace. Even when it feels like nothing more than survival, it's important not to devalue what is being learned through the experience. And one major key I discovered was to never travel the road of transition alone. In my case, as mentioned earlier, I enjoyed my first 18 months on the road with a friend and then, three years later, I was married. Starting new series of revival services every week with a college partner has its challenges, but it was very different from the same type of situation with a life-long companion.

Five years after Lisa and I were married, our first daughter was born and that event produced another huge adjustment. Life on the road was getting really complicated at this point because our child struggled both with allergies and a breathing condition that needed extra care. After struggling with some inadequate accommodations and insensitive hosts, we decided on our next necessary change that proved to be unimaginably beneficial.

We sold our SUV, purchased a diesel suburban, and began pulling a 32-foot Park model travel trailer. I could tell you all kinds of stories about those two years of setting up and tearing down every few days and all the things that happened would keep you entertained indefinitely. The stories would include leaks in the black water lines, dripping roof vents, un-insulated walls, mice, propane malfunctions, automatic locks on the vehicle that required fireman rescue operations, flat tires, wind storms, destroyed awnings, and more. I'll spare you the details and say that RV life on a budget isn't everything it's cracked up to be. If an RV happens to be your primary residence and a part of your livelihood, I commend you and feel for you at the same time.

Answering God's calling has the potential to absolutely scare you to death at times, and remembering my evangelist path reminds me of many of those moments. Getting comfortable is not an option when the very nature of the vocation demands constant fluctuation. But adjusting to new people, ideas, structures, and plans is not something that just happens to evangelists. Many other jobs also require flexibility in transitional phases. Because of that, it's not possible to lay out a simple cut-and-dried plan that should be applied to each one of these unique transitional moments. Instead, it's necessary to approach every transitional situation with a mind that's open to compromise.

My time spent on the road came to a welcomed end when our first baby was 2½ years old. After 10 years on the road, it was time to take on a new challenge.

***

Action Step #30: If you don't have a life partner to travel the road of transition with, look for someone to confide in.

21. Then It Gets Real

There's something valuable to be gained from each of life's vocational experiences.

In March of 1997, Lisa, Madison, and I pulled our travel trailer into Swannanoa, North Carolina to start a brand new church in Asheville. There wasn't anything impressive about the tucked-away, unassuming RV Park that we would camp in for the next eight months. The most picturesque and entertaining thing about this location was the abundance of rabbits filling our unimpressive amount of real estate morning and evening. Our toddler absolutely loved those furry little creatures hopping in every direction each time we stepped out the door or pulled into the drive.

Talk about transition; that first year in western North Carolina was a major adjustment. We were all alone with no congregation or established connections, striking out on a dicey adventure, constantly wondering if things would ever turn out positively. In the following months and before year's end, we started having services in a storefront building and teaching 10-12 Bible studies each week in various homes with our little family. Lisa gave birth to our second daughter, Meghan, in October, and we moved into an upstairs apartment on the backside of a nice complex.

Yes, we were facing transition on three different fronts, a baby, a business, and a bungalow. I would not recommend this path to those with a weak heart. You have to be a little crazy—or confused—to pull it off. We learned countless life lessons during that time and I look back with many fond memories and an appreciation of our dream-filled youth. It helped that we spent our late twenties and early thirties there because, in the ten years we spent in Asheville, we moved six times, including living in an RV, apartment, rental house, and three different homes we built. But that was better than the preceding ten years when we were moving six times every six weeks!

A bold move

What possesses a person to make such a bold move? For us, it had to be the many examples in our life. It is amazing what can happen in a person's life when they are exposed to different opportunities. Lisa and I both saw firsthand, as children watching our parents, what joy can be gained by starting churches and investing in the lives of people. We also had a few friends and family members who were venturing down this same road of church planting. Preaching for them and discussing the ins and outs of this radical endeavor affected us, although, as we discovered, having a feeling about something and wanting it to succeed is much different than actually investing your life into seeing those efforts flourish.

For several years leading up to our church planting attempt, we gave financially to individuals working nationally and internationally in missions. We invested in this type of sacrifice long before it became our own personal reality and since then, more than we ever gave has come back to us, and from many different sources. Jesus said, *"Give, and it shall be given unto you; good measure, pressed down, and shaken together, and running over, shall men give into your bosom. For with the same measure that ye mete withal it shall be measured to you again"* (Luke 6:38). This scriptural principle works. We are living proof.

Building in a graveyard

After receiving a phone call from a state board member of our ministerial organization about starting a church in Asheville, North Carolina, it took nine months of extensive soul-searching to actually accept the challenge. I will never forget what the District Superintendent said when Lisa and I went before their board to gain approval for the endeavor.

His words to us were, "Do you know that Asheville is a graveyard for preachers?" Shocking, but true. We were down a long list of couples who had tried to build a church there, with little success. This was a reality-check like never before! That being the case, I wondered why they contacted *us*? We didn't ask for this impossible task. But he went on to say that the people making the decision believed we would succeed. Thankfully, with God's help, we did accomplish what we set out to do, and the evidence of all that work is the church still in existence and doing well almost twenty years later.

Andy Stanley in his book, *Deep and Wide*, said precisely what I've thought numerous times. A statement on his desk reads, "Lord, this was not my idea, You got me into this. I'm trusting you to see me through it." Yep, I've been there, prayed that, and feel confident I will again. How about you; do you feel the same way? Well, you're not alone!

Taking a "God-risk"

My vocational choice was ramped up exponentially when we decided to transition from evangelist to church planter. Although there are some interchangeable passions, the roles are vastly different. I'm not belittling either ministry pursuit; each has its own joys and trials. With evangelism, you work hard to gain traction and attention in each new location and then reap, in large part, based on the efforts of many in the congregation. In church planting, you're questioned, sometimes overlooked, and usually work alone to produce results. If you know someone who operates in either calling, offer support and encouragement by consistently letting them know how much you appreciate what they are doing.

For my family, the transition from evangelist to church-planter meant canceling between two and three years of upcoming speaking engagements. Our schedule went from jam-packed to empty overnight. That can be unnerving! Along with this, while deciding to start a church from nothing, we turned down opportunities to take the pastorate of five different established churches of varying sizes and geographical locations.

Do you remember that part I mentioned earlier about doors being opened and closed? I have often wondered why it seems that when you take gut-wrenching steps of faith or, as I like to call them, God-risks, you're always tempted with other opportunities. You wonder where those opportunities were when you were struggling along with no options. I've experienced that in every major ministry transition I've made. Don't feel alone if you've experienced the same thing. Over the years, many of those cancelled preaching invitations have resurfaced and opened up again. Because of that, I've enjoyed the option of continuing to fulfill the evangelistic part of my calling, but on a more manageable scale.

Focus on the unseen

Have you heard that saying about leaving the good behind for the great? If not, I recommend reading the book by Jim Collins, called, *Good to Great*. In one sense, this is exactly what I'm talking about. But the "greater" isn't always bigger, brighter, and more beautiful. In fact, it might be the opposite. Understanding this causes you to focus more on the unseen parts of yourself that are being developed by the decision. It's important not to be obsessed with the external shallow view of the situation.

I've stood on the banks of some incredible rivers, viewing the beauty of the location, only to be completely frustrated by the lack of production that came from hours spent trying to catch a fish. But, on the other hand, I've slipped down into a lackluster-looking small mountain stream and immediately hooked up with the fight-of-my-fishing-life on the first cast. The largest brown trout I ever came close to landing, was in one of those exact type of scenarios. I can remember it like yesterday. A buddy and I were fishing the Pink Beds outside of Brevard, North Carolina when I caught a glimpse of a trophy trout under the water's surface right before my initial presentation. Such fun!

Remember, the advantage is being able to detect inwardly what everyone else is missing by just looking on the outward. The Bible says that God does this when he looks at humanity. *"But the Lord said unto Samuel, Look not on his countenance, or on the height of his stature; because I have refused him: for the Lord seeth not as man seeth; for man looketh on the outward appearance, but the Lord looketh on the heart"* (I Samuel 16:7). God observes the inward, the often unseen parts of a person, while man looks on the outside, the more obvious facade. Remember that, in your times of transition.

The complete picture of in, out, and above is the balanced way to move forward in any type of transition. Bright lights mean nothing if there's no substance contained behind the curtain because those same appealing, glowing, attention-getting lights have a way of fading, burning out, and growing dim. Their power comes from somewhere other than themselves. The real source is what's happening elsewhere, hidden, and not easily seen.

A blessing in disguise

So my sweet tenacious wife and I jumped into church-planting with all four feet.

To survive and have a place to live, we started building houses with no prior construction experience. You may think that's nuts, and it probably was, but in a transition, you'll try about anything in order to find stability. My general contracting career started with a book from "Books a Million," called "How to be your own contractor." Those 164-pages covered the basics and helped me gain some knowledge of the process. It sounds wild, thinking back on it now, but it's the truth.

I did get additional encouragement from my father, a couple of friends who had built before, and a complete stranger who I met at Ridgecrest Conference Center in Black Mountain, North Carolina. I met that last guy while looking for a place to host a preacher's kid retreat I was hoping to start at the time. That was a completely different endeavor, eventually materializing and is still in operation today in a different context and location.

The man in that chance encounter ironically became my neighbor because of a piece of property he mentioned to me, right next door to his home. After filling me in on how he had built a few homes including the one he was living in and convincing me that he would help me through the process, he bailed out, once the land was purchased, construction loan secured, and grading began. This was a blessing in disguise, even though it didn't seem like it at the time. Remember, the next time you think there's no way through the transition you're facing and unexpected blows appear, that it's all a part of the process. You are resilient and gifted beyond what others can see on the outside.

I was left hanging, with no real workable knowledge of this type of undertaking, holding nothing more than a degree in Theology! Hey, at least I was in good company. Jesus came to save the world and ended up being a carpenter for the greater part of his 33½ years! Facing a half-graded piece of sloping, impossible property, no help, a construction loan of more than six figures with deadlines and expectations to satisfy, I had no choice but to make this work. I was forced into immediate action!

Sink or swim

Adjusting to the new circumstances and working to remember every lesson I'd learned from all those labor-intensive minimal jobs of my youth, I realized I had to lean on my principles or go under! It's called "sink or swim." I learned that there's something valuable to be gained from each of life's vocational experiences and it's important to be perceptive enough to unearth those benefits. The quickest way to deal with the undeniable pain we all face in transition is to just put your head down and bang it out. There's a reward coming somewhere in life because of your good attitude and good effort.

After successfully building a couple of houses, I finally enrolled in a class to become a licensed General Contractor. This "get-it-done" attitude caused me to be approached by a local businessman who wanted to be the investor of a construction company that he and I would start. My responsibility in the agreement, the "daring risk-taker," was overseeing the construction end. The opportunity came about because I was willing to ask questions of employees and customers at Home Depot, Lowes, Builders Express, subcontractors, hired help, loan officers, tellers, and many other places in our town. In a few years, we had built in different locations, using various architectural designs and on multiple land types. We had to deal with every changing building code and with clueless inspectors. It was a season of life I will always cherish.

For the record, Lisa and I did much of the work, outside of the things requiring specific licenses. We came to the conclusion that purchasing tools and doing some of the work alone would be more productive, time saving, and less of a financial waste. Armed with the advice of others, a few skilled subcontractors, and hired hourly help, we did it!

While the proposed partnership would have provided great financial resources for me personally, it wasn't part of the master plan for my future. This is where the detached, big-picture dimension comes into play. I was in Asheville to build a church, not to build a company, and the church had to remain my priority.

Vocational changes will often come to you out of nowhere. Being able to navigate through them successfully has a lot to do with incorporating your past experiences into the present.

**

Action Step #31: Take a "knowledge and skills" inventory so you know what inner resources you can draw on when faced with a difficult transition.

Action Step #32: Don't try to go-it-alone when learning or transitioning into a new vocation.

22. Yes, That's Another Hat

"Knowing is not enough; we must apply.
Willing is not enough; we must do." —Goethe

Here's what my life has consisted of since 1987: Evangelist, church planter, pastor, builder, mentor, equipper, developer of leaders and men, grad school graduate, speaker, coach, encourager, writer, and more. That list describes almost three decades of my vocational pursuits. In each phase, I was motivated to first seek out and connect with people who had been successful in that particular pursuit. I felt it was necessary to gain insight so I could be prepared to become the best person and worker I could be.

I'm writing in my home office, surrounded by hundreds of books covering various subjects. Believe it or not, I've actually read most of them! There's no possible way to calculate the incredible amount of insight I have gained from each one of them. Many of these titles were recommended by the people I reached out to and they directly address topics applicable to each season of growth.

Knowledge is one thing, but applied knowledge is where the magic happens.

Johann Wolfgang von Goethe presented it this way, "Knowing is not enough; we must apply. Willing is not enough; we must do." Not only do we want to seek out people who have expertise in the field, and take their advice, but we actually need to act on their suggestions. The doing part is key because we will gain necessary experience. But as John C. Maxwell aptly describes in his book, *Failing Forward,* "Experience is not the best teacher, Evaluated experience is the best teacher." This is something I decided to structure my life to accomplish long ago. It's one of the things that keeps me on course. It's imperative for each of us to acquire as much knowledge, experience, truth, principles, techniques, and new discoveries as we can and then apply it all to the current circumstances. If not, then all the preparation time spent will end up being wasted.

Give it away

Author, pastor, and leadership coach Nelson Searcy taught me, along with many others, that true growth is about "learning and returning." It's what every leader should be doing: getting the wisdom, experience, and understanding out of our head and passing it on to others. In my case, seminars, interviews, study, and personal conversations have equipped me to tackle life and the demands placed on me as a minister. I truly desire to be effective in an ever-changing world even if, in some regards, ministry is harder today than at any other time in history.

It's been said that pastoring and starting churches are two of the most difficult and challenging jobs and callings anyone can have. There you go; my unstableness is confirmed, seeing that I have been doing both of those for the last 18 years. Yeah, I have an excuse!

One of the reasons ministry ranks at the top of the list in stressful undertakings is because of the emotional investment it requires. Unlike jobs you can "leave at the office," ministry isn't a vocation that you can ever completely detach from, even though periodic breaks are recommended. In fact taking a vacation or sabbatical is a good thing, but getting away still can't cut the heartstrings of attachment from those you minister to.

Here's a simple way to remember the things I've covered in this chapter so far: F.L.A.G.—**F**ind it, **L**earn it, **A**pply it, and **G**ive it away.

Feelings

When we started the church in Asheville, there was no guarantee that a congregation would materialize or that we would survive the effort. The work of church planting is either a transformational or death process for the founder. This is the only way new life can be birthed. Ask any woman who has experienced childbirth. Carrying the weight and burden of such an important responsibility almost kills you.

Pain, trial, excitement, growth, awkwardness, questions, uncertainties, loss, gain and joy, it's impossible to accurately describe the emotions that accompany the work of church planting. Needless to say, carrying out a startup plan and church launch isn't a breeze. Digging that first church out cost us everything, but when we looked back, a decade later, there was a solid foundation and testimony of diligence and divine favor.

Because of the extreme investment, leaving that effort was one of the most difficult decisions I've made in my entire life. It's not so hard to walk away from people and things when there's a sketchy past, problems, or obvious difficulties brewing. It's almost like poetic justice or a justification. But that wasn't the case when my next pastoral opportunity, yes transition, came.

I really can't describe the feelings tied to that departure. It was excruciating, like experiencing a self-inflicted heart attack. Some transitions feel like your heart is being ripped out of your chest. I remember lying in a hotel room having a panic attack and thinking, "What in the world am I doing?" It wasn't something I could just "get over." Remember, every part of a transition needs to be experienced for ultimate success to happen. My greatest struggle during that time was taking place inwardly.

Pain

For a couple of years after we moved, I couldn't go back to Ashville's Buncombe County without feeling emotionally overwhelmed. In fact, I tried to avoid it all together, even taking the long way around the area so I wouldn't have to drive through the city when on that side of the state. Inadvertently seeing or running into the people from the church caused me to crash inwardly and, at times, outwardly. Even though it was an excruciating departure, deep inside I had to own the belief that it was the right decision for us.

The outward and above parts of the transition went better than the inward ones, and they were navigated without much delay. Selling our home, buying and moving to a city five hours away went off without a hitch. Starting a new routine and living a new schedule happened without much difficulty. Heaven had a new plan for our ministry and the details for arriving at the new church were fairly smooth.

Healing comes

Seven years later we were on a vacation in Tennessee, just a couple hours from Western North Carolina and we decided to drive over and revisit a few places from our past. Riding through Cherokee, Maggie Valley, and Asheville brought back many poignant memories. We stopped by the storefront where we'd first held services, our miracle first church building, the houses we'd built, the apartment we'd lived in, and even the RV Park in Swannanoa where we'd first parked our RV. We ate with friends at our one-time favorite Japanese restaurant, saw people we were acquainted with, drove by ACA (the girls' school), and by places of business we had frequented. It was just like old times, but it felt better this time around. Time had healed the hurt and answered most of the questions.

We'd learned that, although detachment is hard, over time, the other side is better, especially when you get explanation, comfort, reason and resolve. Here's my learned and experienced advice for you: No matter where you are in your transition, don't frustrate yourself by trying to reinvent the wheel. Take the knowledge, experience, and insight of other purposeful travelers and apply it to your own situation.

Best-selling author, Stephen R. Covey wrote, "To learn and not to do is really not to learn. To know and not to do is really not to know."

***

Action Step #33: Get the blessing of all those you have left behind.

23. Never Stop Growing

Personal and professional growth is necessary in transitional times in spite of transition difficulties.

At the age of 46, I went back to school to earn an MA in Christian Leadership. I studied at southern California's Hope International University and Apostolic School of Theology near Sacramento. One of my motivators for more education, beside my personal goal for earning an advanced degree, was that we were relocating to Denver, Colorado to start another church and my research showed that the metro area was a highly-educated area of the country.

An article in the New York Times listed Denver / Aurora / Broomfield, CO as #9 on the list of top 100 metro areas with the most college-educated residents. In 2010, 38.2% of the city's residents held a college degree. I wanted to relate with the educational effort, sacrifice, and commitment of the people living there and provide a shared and mutual respect not available otherwise.

Two degrees, two decades apart

It may sound comical nowadays, but the first time I went to college to earn a BA in Theology, there were no computers, cell phones, Internet, email, or access to learn online or from a distance. Antiquated? Yes! Am I glad things are different today? Absolutely! The world has changed, and in many ways, for the better, however, in spite of it becoming more convenient to earn a graduate degree from a distance, I had to overcome a major technological learning curve. What a challenge to catch up with the advancements of two decades!

After completing those 2½ years of study, I can't adequately explain my feelings of accomplishment. This was due to the fact that I had long questioned parts of my educational experience. As my life had changed, and my knowledge grew, I realized a lack in some areas of my prior learning, which, I'm sure, is the case for everybody after time spent in his or her respective field.

Professional development

Before I jumped into this particular MA pursuit, I committed to three years of leadership coaching with Nelson Searcy and Church Leadership Insights, which focused on specific areas of personal growth and church systems. Unbeknownst to me at the time, I was not only tremendously helped through the challenges I faced in leading an old religious institution through a transition, but it also prepared me for the rigors of a Masters Degree and for starting the church in southeast Aurora, CO.

I felt better prepared this time around than I had 15 years before in Asheville, NC. Not only had I gained a wealth of experiential knowledge, but I had also continued my personal growth and educational efforts while working through many transitions. What, I didn't have a clue about those many years before; I did the second time around. All of that together helped in the planning, strategizing, and structuring of the new church plant, as well as handling the pressures that would come.

After four years in Colorado, we have not only planted one church on the south side of Denver, but recently began a second location on the north side, about 40 minutes away.

Don't assume success

Fear can be eased when the unknown becomes more familiar and then it's easier to be optimistic. However, it's dangerous to feel overly confident and lackadaisical, assuming success will happen just because of your presence. Nothing could be farther from the truth. Successful ventures always require a wholehearted effort along with a clear understanding of the lessons learned from the past. Those two combine to help us to work smarter and with more of an understanding of the potential.

Build your future

If you didn't know this previously, learn it now: personal and professional growth is necessary in transitional times in spite of transition difficulties. Vocational transitions can work out well for you if you take each past experience and invest what you learned into the next opportunity that opens for you. Never stop looking for ways to improve yourself and your skills. And by all means keep reaching for the next level of fulfillment in your career.

If you're not happy with your job, don't just surrender to the misery; make a conscious decision to start working today to build a future that will bring you the reward and contentment you're hoping for. You only have one life to live and your vocation can provide the funds and fulfillment needed to make it great.

The personal vocational highlights I explored in this section all involved transition, and none of them were easy. But, when I look back, I'm pleased to say that I made it through those challenges. And if I did it, there's no doubt in my mind that you can too.

***

Action Step #34: Find out what professional development opportunities are available where you work.

Section V—Spirituality

24. If You're Looking for a Discount, This Isn't the Place

This is the most valuable information I could ever communicate on the subject of transition.

Reverend William T. Cumming said, "There are no atheists in foxholes." Although I've never been there myself, I do know others who can attest to the validity of that statement. Whether you admit it or not, everyone is spiritual to some degree. Before you jump to conclusions thinking I intend to go off on a tangent in the closing portion of this book, please hear me out and be open to how these final ideas may speak to your current reality.

The most important transition

Finally, we focus on the spiritual, which some are willing to address and others discount completely. But recognized or not, it's a real part of the human journey. The truth is, everyone puts trust in someone or something, whether they call it God, a Higher Power, the universe, a statue, a created being, an idol, Presence, or themselves as an evolving deity.

The spiritual part of humanity is the great unknown. It has to do with the elusive present, the questioned future, and the afterlife. Now, please don't worry. I'm not going to give you a zealous argument for "religion in general" but I will share a sincere, upfront revealing of my personal feelings, strength for survival, and hope for tomorrow. Yes, I am all about promoting Jesus Christ and the amazing change that can come into a person's life when they pursue a relationship with Him. But forcing someone beyond his comfort level, to make an eternal decision, isn't my modus operandi.

After reading this far in the book, you should have no questions about where I stand when it comes to faith but I've tried to limit my personal feelings and convictions related to the Bible, God, salvation, or other religious positions. I've only mentioned a few verses, principles, and rock solid foundational truths that have helped me navigate my life's transitions. What I will say in this section, though, is so vital to the entire subject of transition that I decided to make a promise to each person who chooses to read on. Here's the promise: I, Robert Mitchell commit to purposefully not mislead you or to try, in any way, to convert you by having you say a short made-up-on-the-fly prayer. What you do with the material I'll share with you the in next few pages is completely up to you. Deal?

Spiritual Transition

In the next few pages, I'm going to share about how I see spiritual transition and how it relates to the unavoidable reality of every other transition encountered. Of course, there's no pressure to read any farther, but I will say without hesitation, that revelation can come to you at this point like never before! Do you trust me? Will you follow me on the rest of this journey? If so, let's get started. If not, no hard feelings, I promise. I hate to see you go when it's getting so good and I hate that you're going to miss discovering the most important key of all, but I understand.

Thank you for traveling with me. I hope life makes more sense for you now. It's also my sincere desire that you've picked up some tips that will enable you to move forward in your life with clarity. But most of all, I'm glad we've made a connection and I hope my story has helped you to refine your skills in order to successfully navigate the transitions of your own life.

***

Action Step #35: Make a decision to stop reading or to continue.

Don't forget to download my **FREE PDF: "41 Action Steps to Prepare for and Get Through Transition."**

http://transitionbook.info

***

Hey, I'm happy you're still here. Maybe spiritual things appeal to you, maybe not. But one thing is for sure, you've decided to finish what you've started and read to the end of my book. Thank you!

Now that you're continuing on, I hope you won't discount this part, because you may find the answers to many of the questions you had when you first started reading this book. For that matter, even the questions that have developed as a result of the scenarios I presented are going to make sense now. I'll make this one bold declaration and move on, **"You will not be sorry you finished this book."**

I've been going crazy writing hours, days, and months on end, waiting until the end to say these things, because I feel like this is the most valuable information I could ever communicate on the subject of transition. Some of you are so intrigued right now that you're mentally pleading with me to stop talking so you can get to the good stuff. Okay, for your sake and mine, I'll make this final push. Let's go!

25. Everybody Believes In Something

In one form or another, most everyone in the world adheres to a belief in an afterlife or the continuation of existence.

One class I was required to take during my graduate program dealt with the five major world religions. For those who care, the five are: Christianity, Judaism, Islam, Buddhism, and Hinduism. The religion the class spent the least amount of time discussing was Christianity, since most, if not all involved in that study, ascribed to its tenets. A general breakdown of the numbers of people worldwide who adhere to each of the "Big Five" (found on adherence.com), look like this:

- Christianity—2.1 billion

- Islam—1.5 billion

- Hinduism—900 million

- Buddhism—367 million

- Judaism—14 million

As part of the final grade, each student was required to pick one religion, conduct an interview with someone who practiced that religion, and write a paper providing an overall learning, view, and understanding of that religion.

The religion I chose to explore was Islam. It was an interesting study. I enjoyed interviewing an Islamic man and I got an understanding of how to move forward with those immersed in Islamic teachings. One thing I found especially interesting was that, after a few weeks of intense study and exposure to Islam, I was more versed in the teachings than the man I interviewed at the mosque, and he had been raised in it his entire life!

There are few similarities between the five major world religions in spite of what the proponents of universalism would like to admit. People are not all one, coming from various vantage points, walking separate roads that all lead to the same destination and reward. I believe that everyone will, indeed, stand shoulder-to-shoulder one day before the judge of all ages. And there, on that day, these various religious practices will not provide the same outcome.

What happens next?

In one form or another, most everyone in the world adheres to a belief in an afterlife or the continuation of existence. Without going into the details of each of those positions and how they will play out, I'll simply provide these current percentages.

According to theskepticsguide.org, "32% of American Atheists and Agnostics believe in an Afterlife." And with the recent findings of christianpost.com and the Ipsos/Reuters poll, "51% of people in the world believe that there's an afterlife while 23% believe they will just 'cease to exist.' Around a quarter (26%) simply don't know what will happen after death." So, the truth that life does not end at death is widely accepted. And it has been this way for millennia.

As a Christian, I cannot get away from the verse that says, "*And as it is appointed unto men once to die, but after this the judgment*" (Heb. 9:27). **When you and I draw our last breath here on earth, we will immediately inhale eternity's consequences.** What we experience next is a direct result of how our mortal lives were carried out. That's heavy, no matter what position you take! As I heard one minister say, some 30 years ago, "If I'm wrong, I'm still right." In other words, if, by chance, it doesn't turn out exactly like I mentioned above, then what have I lost? Nothing. But if it's the truth, then every conforming choice I made was absolutely worth it.

The teachings, acceptance—and often misrepresentation—of an afterlife are prevalent in the world. Neither education nor affluence can change this reality. Nothing—not color, race, ethnicity, social status, age, generation, wealth, location, nor era—will alter the result.

***

Action Step #36: Ask yourself, "What do I believe about the hereafter?" Why do I believe it that way? Write down the answer.

26. No Boring Bible Study Here

The Bible is filled with examples of transition in ministry from one generation and leader to the next.

The concept of transition is found throughout the Bible. If I were to explore every one of those transitions, this book would exponentially increase in size. Because of that, I have chosen to highlight just a few of the more recognizable ministerial and spiritual transitions.

Hannah, Samuel, and Eli

One transition that stands out in the Old Testament is the dramatic hand off between Eli and Samuel. Eli was a high priest in Israel and enjoyed a rather long tenure. But not everything about his leadership was commendable. Under his leadership, God's people went into moral decay and severe spiritual decline. Unfortunately, Eli wasn't able to do much about this tragic collapse or turn the heart of Israel back toward God. Further, his sons showed such disregard for the holy things and were so sinful that God didn't allow Eli to pass the priestly role to them. Instead, God provided a completely different candidate to fill that position, one who would put God first.

In case you're not familiar with the story from I Samuel 1-4, let me catch you up:

The story begins with an infertile woman named Hannah who begs the Lord to bless her with a son. She promises God that, if he answers her prayer, she will give that answered prayer back to God for service in his house. Over time, this is exactly what happened. Out of this fulfilled commitment, an amazing example of transition develops.

Hannah took her young son Samuel and presented him to Eli, to serve in God's house, and that's where he grew up. At the end of Eli's life, the new spiritual voice of Israel becomes Hannah's son instead of the position transitioning to one of Eli's corrupt sons. Samuel assumed the duties of high priest and also became the inaugural prophet in that great land. The significance of this transition cannot be ignored.

Often in the supernatural realm, things happen in times of transition that literally change the whole context of your life, which, in turn, affects others. Eli and Samuel's transition included sacrifice, development, commitment, sensitivity, learning, change, difficulty and excitement—all kinds of amazing things! If you're not currently experiencing all these, don't worry, they may be just around the corner! Meanwhile, it's okay if several things are happening all at once. They may be introducing something new and transformational to your life and ministry.

Elijah and Elisha

The next transition story we're going to look at involves Elijah and Elisha from I Kings 19 to II Kings 2. The stories of Bible transitions from one prophet to another never lose their appeal and this one is no exception. It really could've turned out vastly differently, but it didn't and, interestingly, never does.

Elijah, a chosen man of God anticipates the end of his ministry and effectiveness so he sets out, by direction of God, to find a successor. He doesn't leave this obligation to chance. When he finds Elisha, an unsuspecting young man with the potential for greatness, Elijah casts his mantel on Elisha's shoulders. Right in the middle of carrying out his everyday responsibilities, Elisha experiences a moment when Heaven's limitlessness intersects with a human's limits. For my fellow AST Christian Leadership graduates, as Dr. Nathaniel J. Wilson teaches, "the kairos suddenly breaking into the chronos, dramatically instituting personal realignment."

It would be nice to know the backdrop of Elisha's story. The only thing we know, from the surrounding verses and context, is that he was actively living his life. This young man wasn't idly waiting for something phenomenal to occur; he was just intently working to move his life forward in a productive way.

Many times, when beneficial transitions take place in our lives, it's because of a refusal to sit any longer in mind-numbing boredom. Those who pour their best efforts into their present obligations are often surprised by what comes out of it. Opportunity always finds the person who senses it's time for a change, the one who pursues favor in every moment, and the individual who remains faithful in their current set of responsibilities.

After their initial encounter, Elijah and Elisha form a relationship based on mutual respect. Elijah makes a promise and Elisha makes a commitment. Honestly, this is all that can be expected in similar arrangements and neither knew if the other would keep his word. In this case, it worked, and a double portion of the elder's anointing was granted to the younger. Elisha's unwavering faithfulness put him into position to receive his request.

Do you wonder if things will ever go to another level for you and if you will ever get your turn on ministry's stage? The story of this transition should cause a paradigm shift in your thinking because it reveals foresight, release, confidence, focus, trust, and unwavering support.

Jesus Christ

The New Testament saga of Jesus Christ and his disciples unequivocally details the most important handoff in human existence. No, I'm not overstating this or bordering on hyperbole. Nothing in history—past, present, or future—even begins to compare to the importance of this transaction. Christ comes into the world through the womb of a teenage girl, shrouded with question. His birth was not without purpose. In fact, an angel declared the purpose even before Jesus was born with the proclamation, "*And she shall bring forth a son, and thou shalt call his name Jesus: for he shall save his people from their sins*" (Matt 1:21). The incarnation amazes me. Deliverance exploded on the scene of captivity.

Jesus' purpose was sacrifice and redemption and to accomplish this, he had to travel many difficult roads, either physically, emotionally or mentally. Along the way, he found men who would follow his path and develop a similar passion. **Exposure is the best asset for connecting people to greater endeavors.** Jesus exposed his chosen disciples, from various walks of life and vocations, to a cause that would ultimately arrest their attention and determine the actions of the rest of their lives. Even though watching him face execution rocked their private worlds, it couldn't dislodge them from their called purpose. After his resurrection and approaching ascension, he literally handed them the reason for his death.

Imagine the responsibility these disciples felt when Jesus went away! I can't think of a comparison that comes even remotely close. The future of human salvation rested on the shoulders of these frail, susceptible, common men, but they embraced the challenge and turned their world upside down. "*And when they found them not, they drew Jason and certain brethren unto the rulers of the city, crying, These that have turned the world upside down are come hither also*" (Acts 17:6).

This transition is possibly the hardest one in Scripture to understand and rationalize. God took a chance on the creation he had fashioned with his own hands. "*And the Lord God formed man of the dust of the ground, and breathed into his nostrils the breath of life; and man became a living soul*" (Gen. 2:7). This transition speaks of confidence, risk, question, loss, victory, shock, rejoicing, betrayal, forgiveness, and redemption.

Paul

Then the next generation of spiritual leaders arrived—individuals like Saul (who became Paul), along with those who followed him. A murderer turned missionary ... what a story of grace, forgiveness, and mercy!

Three recorded journeys later, many people were converted and others were brought close and trained as spiritual leaders to carry the cause forward. Paul wrote letters, established churches, survived attacks and endured tests, then, at the end of his life, you find, arguably, the greatest apostle of all saying, "*For I am now ready to be offered, and the time of my departure is at hand. I have fought a good fight, I have finished my course, I have kept the faith: Henceforth there is laid up for me a crown of righteousness, which the Lord, the righteous judge, shall give me at that day: and not to me only, but unto all them also that love his appearing*" (II Timothy 4:6-8). Such amazing words, especially when taking into consideration the trials he faced, the difficulties he overcame and the responsibilities he shouldered.

Somehow, by the grace of God, Paul endured those things with honor and understanding, or no one would have been willing to follow in his footsteps. Many of his sons in the gospel embraced the transition of Paul's ministry and went forward with it. If destiny, calling, and purpose are internalized, nothing can thwart beneficial transition, not despair, trial, sickness, abandonment, relocation, instability, uncertainty, rejection, or anything else.

Why is it so hard?

The Bible is filled with examples of transition in ministry from one generation and leader to the next. It makes me wonder why, in many of today's Christian leadership circles, ministerial transition is one of the most difficult, cutthroat, untrusting, and unhealthy environments in society? Sadly, there are too many horror stories of present-day pastoral transitions going bad. My observation is that the most common causes for ministry transition failure are rooted in feelings of possessiveness, pride, and superiority. I probably shouldn't state it so strongly without taking adequate time to make a case for this viewpoint, but I'll take the risk and leave it right there. There's no animosity here, just a simple view from a person with a lifetime of exposure to ministry's ups and downs.

I should mention that the type of ministry I'm referring to here is when a minister is actually called by God into this vocation—not a "best option" career path chosen in some seminary. This is a completely different undertaking than anything I've previously discussed. When you understand this, you immediately realize that eternity is at stake, both for the minister and for those to whom he or she is appointed. It isn't easy to walk away from, or hand-off a ministry because you've been involved in life-saving measures and, even greater, eternity-altering efforts.

Retiring from active, lifelong ministry is an oxymoron and practically impossible. It would be like taking a person's heart out of their chest and expecting them to actually go on living. Because of that, it's wonderful to hear when a ministerial transition is accomplished successfully without hurt, misunderstanding, jealousy, fallout, and collateral damage. Getting it right is of paramount importance to the church and shouldn't be feared. Making preparation well in advance, along with discovering the next door of ministry opportunity, is the most advantageous approach. In certain situations it comes down to the ability to see the reward waiting on the other side of the challenging change. Fulfillment can be realized in new ministry paths chosen.

Business transitions

It's only fair to point out that this type of vulnerability is not just in religious circles. Reading through the leadership transitions of various companies like Coke, Microsoft, Southwest Airlines, Apple, Ritz Carlton, IBM, Shell Oil, Bank of America, Chrysler, and many others, reveals that even major conglomerates have their share of difficult transitions. Yet after decades of economic ups and downs, they succeed. It comes down to the wherewithal and willingness to adjust, regroup, right the ship, cast renewed vision, and move forward.

Transition is a difficult but necessary aspect of every department and at each level of those companies. It isn't just found at the top. Sometimes, things go well and the general public hears nothing about it, and, at other times, a bump in the road happens and the world is made aware.

Often, in the middle of transitions, you're not sure if the company will make it, but in time, balance comes back and things smooth out. If not, the businesses I mentioned earlier would've gone out of business decades ago. Looking at the collective number of years and international events those businesses have survived is a testimony that transition doesn't have to be a death sentence but an opportunity to grow even larger. Peter Drucker, a leading business mind, stated, "Once a company reaches 30% effectiveness or accomplishment, it is time to tear it down and restructure or the next wave of growth will be forfeited." Truly successful companies are those that are in a constant place of transitional purpose. Those who are willing to initiate transition before others realize the need for it, enjoy strength and longevity.

Sports transitions

Then there's the world of professional sports. Who has time to keep up with the constant transitions surrounding that market? From the outside, it sounds like a perpetual merry-go-round for even the most talented athletes. No wonder so many individuals involved in the sports rat race find themselves making the headlines for things they would rather not be known for.

There appears to be no loyalty, lasting respect, or appreciation for efforts given or time spent. It's a sad picture of transitions that never end well nor bring benefit to those involved. And if there's any accomplishment or achievement, it's so short lived, which makes the participants wonder if it was worth all the sacrifices they made. Think about all the coaches, players, contracts, names, cities, endorsements, colors, uniforms, sponsors, arenas, stadiums, promotions, heroes, lawsuits, litigations, unions, mascots, critics, haters, and rules that are always susceptible to change. It makes my head and heart hurt for those who give themselves to the process. The bright spots are few in comparison to the train wrecks that consistently surface.

Transitions in medicine

What about the examples of professionals in the field of medicine? It was virtually impossible to grow up in Houston and not have some awareness of the Texas Medical Center and its increasing influence. Two names were synonymous with medical breakthroughs and cutting-edge cardiac procedures: Drs. Michael E. DeBakey and Denton A. Cooley. These men, both consummate professionals dealing directly with the heart issues, were pace-setters in their field of research, procedure, care, and treatment.

Consider all the medical professionals who studied and practiced under them. Teams of qualified, highly skilled, trained, and educated individuals were there with them every step of the way. Attempting transition in that field seems to come at a higher cost because of the life and death risk involved. It would be hard to calculate the lives saved and futures extended by the work DeBakey, Cooley, and their teams accomplished. Yet, control had to be relinquished and transition completed in order for medical breakthroughs to continue.

Transition comes to the most important areas of life, business, and careers, which means that many others in society understand the pressures you now face. But what matters more than anything else is the productive changes that occur in the spiritual part of you.

***

Action Step #37: Think of your life as a Fortune 500 company and draw a chart of your growth—not just financially but also emotionally, educationally, and spiritually.

Action Step #38: Decide to whom you will pass on your mantle or spiritual passions?

27. Lessons Learned at a Funeral

Transition is a miracle!

In the spring of 2014, I traveled with my wife to the home-going service of a close friend's father. This man was highly respected among his peers and community. He labored for many years in gospel ministry and gained a following of young and old alike. The events surrounding his memorial service were amazing and it was our honor to support his family in their time of grief.

While preparing to write this book, I obsessively compiled information, thoughts, and a plethora of resources to adequately transmit my feelings on the subject. During that particular funeral service, several speakers graced the platform and spoke encouraging words to the family and shared humorous stories about this bigger-than-life man.

Then a gifted minister and long-time friend of the deceased started to speak, and I was instantly caught up in his way of easing the crowd and weaving complimentary words into this moment of sorrow. Then he began to pray, referencing the "miracle of transition," and, just like that, my attention shifted to another level, simply because of where my mind and heart had been while birthing this book.

The exact words he used escape me now, but here's what I took away from those brief but poignant minutes.

Transition is a miracle! And the transition from this life into the next is the final move you will make. To me, this is the most incredible transition of all and if you get this one wrong, you'll have all of eternity to pay. That is serious business. But, if you get it right, it will prove to be the greatest accomplishment of your entire existence.

I picked up an unforgettable lesson about the miracle of transition that day through the words and prayer of Paul Mooney about his friend, Frank Munsey. I have carried them with me since that moment and I trust you will too.

What's the real purpose of life's transitions?

Here's a thought. Could all of life's transitions be for the purpose of preparing you for that coming, Heavenly event? If so, you can't afford to avoid the hard moments life brings or you might not be prepared to face that final transition. It comes down to this, "If you're living the easy life now, it will be hard then. But if you're living hard now, it will be easy then!"

Before that final change you need to transition from spiritual death to spiritual life. This is the greatest transition you can experience on earth. This shift is what the Bible calls the "new birth" or being "born again." But the real result of that supernatural event is realized when the ultimate change happens in that gap between time-bound life and eternity. This transition happens suddenly, literally a split second occurrence.

I've been waiting this entire book to share this reality, "*Beloved, now are we the sons of God, and it doth not yet appear what we shall be: but we know that, when he shall appear, we shall be like him; for we shall see him as he is*" (I John 3:2). Amazing, right? Trying to wrap your brain around that truth is a never-ending quest. And I'm not ever going to stop trying.

This is what all other transitions in life are all about. Every transition we navigate through prepares us for this final and most important one.

We are being led, whether we realize it or not, toward this culmination of all personal, vocational, relational, and spiritual transitions.

***

Action Step #39: Prepare for the transition of death.

28. It Boils Down to This

Stay diligent in working to maintain the right perspective and understanding of your life purpose.

Transition starts out early in life with the objective of leading you to a relationship with Jesus Christ and then to the ultimate transition from mortality to immortality.

"In a moment, in the twinkling of an eye, at the last trump: for the trumpet shall sound, and the dead shall be raised incorruptible, and we shall be changed. For this corruptible must put on incorruption, and this mortal must put on immortality. So when this corruptible shall have put on incorruption, and this mortal shall have put on immortality, then shall be brought to pass the saying that is written, Death is swallowed up in victory" (I Corinthians 15:52-54). The change that Paul was talking about here had to do with the final transition for all humanity. And it's one that, once it begins, you can then do nothing to reverse it.

It's impossible to tell you the exact day, hour or second this will happen. It's beyond our ability to know. For this reason, it's imperative that you live every day, hour, and second as though it were THE moment. When you view it from this vantage point, it's much easier to walk through difficult times. It also heightens the absolute need to keep going and not to quit in the process or give up in the journey.

Learning and gaining everything possible from painful, uncomfortable, and heartbreaking experiences is paramount.

I'll sum up transition like this: the ability to find significance in every stage of life and navigate every circumstance with reassured destiny.

There's no way to say this any better than the way Leo F. Buscaglia stated it, "The person who risks nothing, does nothing, has nothing, is nothing, and becomes nothing. He may avoid suffering and sorrow, but he simply cannot learn and feel and change and grow and love and live."

Finally...

Here's the BIG takeaway, Stay diligent in working to maintain the right perspective and understanding of your life purpose. If you can somehow realize, through what you have learned in this book or as a result of the things you have already faced, that your life is important and there's a determined reason for the many life transitions you've experienced, then you have hope for better tomorrows. And what will be the reality for the spiritually in-tune individual? A reward that's out of this world!

***

Action Step #40: Evaluation of experience is the greatest teacher, so examine all the painful, uncomfortable, and heartbreaking experiences from your transitions.

Action Step #41: Pray and meditate on your life purpose and what God has in store for you.

Conclusion—Approach Transition with Resolve

Everyone—even you—is affected by transition.

For several years after moving to Colorado, people would ask us if we had visited the southwestern part of the state, including Telluride, Durango, Silverton, Four Corners, and Mesa Verde. Our answer was always the same, "Not yet, but we plan to." Finally, after all the questions, our family was able to take a quick, three-day trip to the Western Slope of our state. It was summer, the kids were out of school, and we had some time to spare in the middle of the week, so we struck out on this new adventure. (For the record, three days wasn't long enough, since we were traveling by car from Denver, six or seven hours away.)

Even though it was a quick trip, it was awesome! We saw breathtakingly beautiful views and enjoyed new experiences. The highlight was visiting the ancient cliff dwellings at Mesa Verde National Park and learning about the several-hundred-year historical journey of the Ute Indians. Our youngest daughter Marley was especially captivated. We were able to observe the progression and development of the Pueblo cliff dwellers and I could see, played out throughout those amazing cliffs that have survived so long, that life is always in a state of flux.

It couldn't have been an easy feat for these people to migrate from the lowlands to a higher plateau in order to improve their lives. When they first arrived in their new location, they dug shallow holes in the earth to live in. Later, they added makeshift roofs, and, eventually, they honed out deeper crevasses and expanded into sections to accommodate fires for warmth and cooking. Then they constructed dwellings and established communities in the sides of the rock walls.

Precarious handholds to climb up and down the cliffs provided access to hunting and agriculture above. Archeologists believe that one unfinished temple project required the help of an estimated 600 or more people. But after several hundred years of vibrant existence, the cliff dwellings were abandoned because of climate fluctuations, and the people moved somewhere else. Obviously, transition is not just a twenty-first-century happening. It has taken place perpetually throughout the ages.

There's nothing static about life. Everyone—even you—is affected by transition. The truth is, life is simply about moving from one transition to the next. If you've just finished one transition, know that another is just around the corner. To live a full and rewarding life, embrace this truth and don't ignore it or try to run from it. Remember that we only get one chance to successfully travel through life so let's make the best of that single opportunity.

And no matter how many you experience, transitions never get easier. It couldn't have been easy for the native peoples of Mesa Verde to make the decision to move on from the familiar and comfortable place they'd settled in, but I like to imagine that they approached the transition with a settled resolve and a hope that their future would be better. Similarly, when you're stuck in an unproductive place, the only healthy option is to accept that a transition is necessary and to move forward with resolve.

Instead of being fearful and apprehensive about tomorrow, choose to go into each new season confident that, by employing purposeful action, you will come through it better. No matter what life brings, there is a way through.

***

Visit http://transitionbook.info to download my FREE PDF: "41 Action Steps to Prepare for and Get Through Transition."

Recommended Reading

Boundaries by Henry Cloud and John Townsend

Deep and Wide by Andy Stanley

Failing Forward by John C. Maxwell

Good to Great by Jim Collins

Halftime by Bob Buford

How To Be Your Own Contractor by Gene and Katie Hamilton

Ignite by Mitch Matthews

Life in a Glass House by Cameron Lee and Jack Balswick

Life Is a Marathon by Bruce Van Horn

Making Room for Life by Randy Frazee

Ordering Your Private World by Gordon McDonald

Outliers by Malcolm Gladwell

Soulprint: Discovering Your Divine Destiny by Mark Batterson

The Bible

The Rhythm of Life by Richard Exley

The Top Five Regrets of the Dying by Bronnie Ware

What on Earth Am I Here For by Rick Warren

Acknowledgments

No project like this can be completed without thanking and acknowledging so many who helped me in my quest to become a self-published author. Space leaves me room to name just a few of them here.

First and foremost, I want to give a huge thank-you to my wonderful wife Lisa, who encouraged me for several years to write a book. Babe, I'm certain transition was not the topic you thought I would tackle first.

Additionally, my heartfelt appreciation goes to:

Joseph Michael my Scrivener guru, who ultimately connected me with Chandler Bolt and Self Publishing School. I would not have accomplished this without Chandler's influence and the step-by-step process SPS provides. Also, out of that introduction, many friendships were established with my fellow students, writers, and authors. (If you have ever thought about writing a book and plan on checking it off your bucket list at some point, I highly recommend making Self Publishing School a major part of that process. Just follow this url for more information.

https://xe172.isrefer.com/go/video1/RobertMitchell2

Megan Jamison, my SPS coach.

Angelique Mroczka, my formatter.

Ida Fia Sveningsson, my cover and back page designer.

Michael Moore, my accountability partner.

Wayne Purdin, my initial editor.

Karen Hemmes, my reality check, rewrite, and reorganization editor, along with the bio and book description creator.

Ronnie Ingle, my legal advisor.

My Launch team and prerelease readers.

Joy Haney, Steve Pixler, Todd Nichols, and Eugene Wilson—fellow authors who each gave me a few minutes of their precious time as I began this endeavor.

All of you who patiently waited for this release you thought would never come.

And last, but not least, my Savior, Jesus Christ, the Only God.

About the Author

Prolific speaker, minister, church planter, husband, father, and adventurer, **Robert Mitchell** writes about transitions from a wealth of personal life experiences.

Born in Houston, Texas and raised in a home filled with love, acceptance, encouragement, and vision, he has lived in five states, visited every state, major city, most national parks and notable landmark in the United States, and traveled throughout the Americas, Europe and Asia. He has spoken or facilitated in over 10,000 events with audiences from one to thousands, in a variety of venues.

Holding a Master's Degree in Leadership, and continually reading, learning, and investing in ongoing personal development, Robert has taught, coached, lead, advised, and given guidance to hundreds of individuals through the changes and obstacles they've faced.

Robert's ministry passion is in evangelism and church planting, having personally started three works and mentoring other leaders in additional new ministries. Robert and his wife Lisa currently live in Colorado, where he pastors two startup churches. He and Lisa are parents to three daughters—two in college and one still at home.

For more information please visit, http://transitionbook.info

Social media whereabouts:

- Twitter: @RobertMitchell2

- Facebook: Robert Mitchell II

- LinkedIn: Robert Mitchell

Made in the USA
San Bernardino, CA
27 March 2020

66417615R00091